I0374679

Twelve Essential Upanishads

Volume III

Taittiriya, Aitareya, Kaushitaki, Kena, Katha, Isha, Shvetashvatara, Mundaka, Prashna, & Mandukya Upanishads

Twelve Essential Upanishads

Three Volume Series

English translation with annotations

Shukavak N. Dasa

ISBN 978-1-889756-00-4

Volume I

Brihad Aranyaka Upanishad:
The Forest Teachings

Volume II

Chandogya Upanishad:
Teachings from the High Chant

Volume III

Taitiriya, Aitareya, Kaushitaki,
Kena, Katha, Isha, Shvetashvatara,
Mundaka, Prashna, & Mandukya
Upanishads

ISBN 978-1-889756-33-2

ISBN 978-1-889756-04-2

Twelve Essential Upanishads

Volume III

Taittiriya, Aitareya, Kaushitaki, Kena, Katha, Isha, Shvetashvatara, Mundaka, Prashna, & Mandukya Upanishads

Translation and Annotations

Shukavak N. Dasa

SRI PUBLICATIONS
SANSKRIT RELIGIONS INSTITUTE
LOS ANGELES

SRI Publications
Sanskrit Religions Institute
www.sanskrit.org
SAN 299-2892

LCCN 2024946386
ISBN 978-1-889756-07-3 (Hardcover)
ISBN 978-1-889756-04-2 (Paperback)
ISBN 978-1-889756-08-0 (EPUB)

Acknowledgements

I thank Dr. Vijay Arora, Ash and Nita Patel, Archana and Akhil Sheth, and Vikas Sharma and family for their generous support publishing these volumes. I also thank Robert Arconti for editing and proofreading, along with Sukulina Dasi for layout, book design, and indexing.

About the Author

Shukavak N. Dasa holds a Ph.D. in South Asian Studies and a Master's degree in Sanskrit grammar from the University of Toronto. He regularly lectures on Hinduism and has played a key role in the development of Hindu temples across the United States and Canada.

He has officiated thousands of Hindu weddings and performed a wide range of rituals in North America, Europe, and India. With deep knowledge of Sanskrit and the symbolic meaning behind Hindu rites, Shukavak is known for making complex traditions accessible and enlightening for diverse audiences—including both lifelong practitioners and those new to the faith.

This translation was undertaken by a Westerner who is also a dedicated practitioner of Hinduism. With a nuanced understanding of the distinction between faith and belief, and drawing from his Western education and personal spiritual practice, the author approaches these sacred texts with both reverence and a desire to find meaning relevant to a Western context. His unique perspective bridges two worlds: rooted in Western thought, yet deeply engaged with Indian spiritual traditions. www.Shukavak.com

A Note on Transliteration and Italicization

The English alphabet has twenty-six basic written sounds. The Sanskrit alphabet has forty-six basic written sounds. That's twenty additional sounds that English does not have, which are expressed by twenty different letters. So when we try to match the sounds of one alphabet to another, if there are not enough letters to make this match, we employ a system of diacritical marks to extend the range of the smaller alphabet. For example, English has just one "a" sound. Sanskrit has three "a" sounds. So to extend the letter "a," we add two separate diacritical marks. In this way we get "a" plus two additional "a" sounds, "ā" and "ā3." Similarly, English has one sibilant, "s," whereas Sanskrit has three sibilants. In this way we get "s" plus "ṣ" and "ś". Additionally, Sanskrit has four nasal sounds while English has only one. In this way we get "n" plus "ñ," "ṅ" and "ṇ." And there are more sounds that employ diacritics, and naturally each diacritical notation has a slightly different pronunciation.

A good example of how this actually works is with the word Krishna. Properly expressed using diacritical notation, this word should be written as Kṛṣṇa. The anglicization "Krishna" is just an approximation of the sound expressed by the diacritical notation Kṛṣṇa. But who can understand the sounds created with diacritical marks without proper training? It is a difficult matter.

In this publication, in order to simplify the words for the non-technical reader, we have elected to not use diacritical notation in the case of book titles and proper names. Consequently, Ṛg Veda has become Rig Veda, the name Gārgī has become Gargi, Īśopaniṣad becomes Isha Upanishad, etc. The one notable exception is with the words *brahma* and Brahmā. When this distinction comes up, it is explained in the annotation. Following this standard we have hopefully made it easier for the non-technical reader to at least pronounce proper names and titles. Otherwise, the standard use of diacritical marks has been employed for all words that are not proper names or book titles.

As far as italicization is concerned, generally book titles are italicized. In this publication, however, in order to streamline the text, which already has so many italicized Sanskrit words, I have elected not to italicize the titles of books.

Table of Contents

Abbreviations xii

Introduction to the Upanishads xiii

1. Taittiriya Upanishad..1

Śikṣāvallī Vallī..6

Ānanda-Vallī 17

Bhṛgu-vallī 27

2. Aitareya Upanishad 33

First *Adhyāya* Creation..35

Second *Adhyāya* Birth..41

Third *Adhyāya* The *Ātmā* 42

3. Kaushitaki Upanishad..45

First *Adhyāya* 47

Second *Adhyāya* 55

Third *Adhyāya* 69

Fourth *Adhyāya* 76

4. Kena Upanishad....................................85
First *Khaṇḍa* 87
Second *Khaṇḍa* 89
Third *Khaṇḍa* 90
Fourth *Khaṇḍa* 93

5. Katha Upanishad......................................95
First *Vallī* Dialogue with Death...........................97
Second *Vallī* 103
Third *Vallī*..109
Fourth *Vallī* 113
Fifth *Vallī* 115
Sixth *Vallī* 119

6. Isha Upanishad.......................................125

7. Shvetashvatara Upanishad................................135
First *Adhyāya* 137
Second *Adhyāya* 143
Third *Adhyāya* 147
Fourth *Adhyāya* 151
Fifth *Adhyāya* 156
Sixth *Adhyāya* 159

8. Mundaka Upanishad.......................................165
First *Muṇḍaka* 167
Second *Muṇḍaka* 173
Third *Muṇḍaka* 179

9. Prashna Upanishad..185
First *Praśna* 187
Second *Praśna* 190
Third *Praśna* 193
Fourth *Praśna* 197
Fifth *Praśna* 200
Sixth *Praśna* 202

10. Mandukya Upanishad......................................205
Om and the Four States of Awareness..............................207

Sanskrit Glossary 211
Index 221

Abbreviations

AU Aitareya Upanishad
BG Bhagavad Gita
BU Brihad Aranyaka Upanishad
ChU Chandogya Upanishad
IU Isha Upaniṣad
KauU Kaushitaki Upanishad
KeU Kena Upanishad
KU Katha Upanishad
MB Mahabharata
MaiU Maitri Upanishad
ManU Mandukya Upanishad
MS Manu Samhita
MuU Mundaka Upanishad
PU Prashna Upanishad
R Ramayana
RV Rig Veda
SK Sankhya Karika
SU Shvetashvatara Upanishad
TA Taitiriya Aranyaka
TU Taitiriya Upanishad
VS Vasishtha Smriti

Introduction to the Upanishads

Reading an ancient document is like looking through the lens of a powerful telescope. The light that reaches the telescope has traveled huge distances before it finally reaches the lens of the telescope and eye of the observer. This light may be thousands of light years old, and so the observer is looking at the way things were at the time the light first began its journey. One is truly looking back in time! Similarly, the text of an ancient document is a snapshot of how things were at the time the particular document was composed. These Upanishads are ancient religious documents first composed thousands of years ago, and therefore, as we read them, we are looking back in time, seeing the state of religious thinking and practice in India at that time. The word *upaniṣad* refers to an esoteric or secret doctrine and so these Upanishads are a collection of ancient mystical teachings from a very ancient time.

The religious writings of Hinduism are collectively grouped under what is called the Vedas. The word *veda* just means "knowledge." The word is derived from the Sanskrit root *vid,* meaning "to know." So the Vedas are literally the knowing of ancient India. Today these Vedas are in two parts, the Shruti Vedas and the Smriti Vedas. We might call these two divisions the "really, really old," and the "just old." The Shruti Vedas are described as *a-pauruṣeya,* whereas the Smriti Vedas are described as *pauruṣeya*. The word *pauruṣeya* means "man-made" and *a-pauruṣeya* means "not man-made." Man-made means writings that were composed and written by a human being. These include such writings as the Mahabharata, the Ramayana, and the many Puranas. Various human writers, such as Vyasa, Valmiki and Badarayana, are the traditional authors credited with composing and recording these Smriti Vedas. The Shruti Vedas, on the other hand, have no such human authors. They are described as works that were "heard" in the hearts of semi-divine beings known as *ṛṣis*. Generally, the Shruti Vedas command higher authority than the Smriti Vedas, even though most of modern Hinduism follows the Smriti Vedas. Consequently, the stories of Rama and Sita, including the life of Hanuman, and the words of Krishna in the Bhagavad Gita are all part of the Smriti Vedas. So too are the stories of Shiva, Parvati, Ganesha and Durga.

The Upanishads fall within the purview of the Shruti Vedas and therefore hold the highest authority. The foundations of the Shruti Vedas are the four Vedas: Rig, Yajur, Sama and Atharva. Each of these four Vedas are divided into four branches called *śakhas*: the *chandas*, the *brāhmaṇas*, the *araṇyakas*, and the *upaniṣads*. Therefore, each Upanishad is connected to one of these four Vedas. Thus, some Upanishads are connected to the Rig Veda while others are connected to the Yajur Veda, the Sama Veda or the Atharva Veda.

In general, over a hundred Upanishads are known, of which just over a dozen or so are considered the oldest and most important.

These are called the principal (*mukhya*) Upanishads. Many Upanishads are later and some are even considered apocryphal. These later Upanishads, numbering about ninety-five, are often referred to as minor Upanishads and are dated from the first millennium CE right up until the fourteenth century CE. Commentators such as Shankara and Madhva have written commentaries on just ten of the principal Upanishads, but it is common to see publications of eleven, thirteen and eighteen Upanishads. The present publication presents twelve such principal Upanishads.

These principal Upanishads were traditionally memorized and passed down orally and are considered to predate the Common Era. Unfortunately, there is no scholarly consensus on their actual date or even which ones are pre- or post-Buddhist. The Brihad Aranyaka is seen as particularly ancient by current scholarship and therefore considered the oldest.

Patrick Olivelle, a Sanskrit philologist and Indologist, gives the following chronology for these principal Upanishads:

> The Brihad Aranyaka and the Chandogya are the two earliest Upanishads. They are edited texts, some of whose sources are much older than others. The two texts are pre-Buddhist; they may be placed in the seventh to sixth centuries BCE, give or take a century or so.
>
> The three other early prose Upanishads—Taittiriya, Aitareya, and Kausitaki— come next; all are probably pre-Buddhist and can be assigned

> to the sixth to fifth centuries BCE.
>
> The Kena is the oldest of the verse Upanishads, followed by the Katha, Isha, Shvetasvatara and Mundaka. All these Upanishads were composed probably in the last few centuries BCE.
>
> The two late prose Upanishads, the Prashna and the Mandukya, cannot be much older than the beginning of the common era.

These older principal Upanishads have naturally inspired a vast commentary tradition, the most important of which are the commentaries of Shankara Acharya, whose date is generally accepted around 700 CE. Shankara wrote many works during his lifetime, perhaps the most important of which are his commentaries on ten of the principal Upanishads, his Bhagavad Gita commentary and his Brahma Sutra commentary. These are the so-called *prasthāna-trayi,* or three foundational works that form the basis of *vedānta* theology.

Vedānta was an attempt to forge a synthesis and thereby find a "final conclusion" (*siddhānta*) to the Vedas, including both the Shruti Vedas and the Smriti Vedas. It was an early attempt to unify and smooth out the contradictions within the Vedas. Shankara's version of this Vedanta is known as *advaita*, but other commentators, such as Ramanuja (circa 1050 CE) and Madhva (circa 1200 CE), have their own schools of *vedānta*, also based on the *prasthāna-trayi,* known respectively as *vaśiṣṭhādvaita* and *dvaita*. Shankara's Advaita Vedanta by far holds the greatest popularity. Many followers of *vedānta* think that *vedānta* means Advaita Vedanta. They may not know there are competing forms of *vedānta*, that Madhva's Dvaita Vedanta is diametrically opposed to Shankara's Advaita Vedanta or that both synthesize a form of *vedānta* out of the very same *prasthāna-trayi* used by Shankara. They may not realize, for example, that the famous dictum *tat tvam asi* (that you are), which Shankara so commonly quotes, can also be legitimately read as *a-tat tvam asi* (that you are not), as Madhva reads this dictum.

Unfortunately, the intense impact of Shankara and the subsequent commentators following in his line of Advaita Vedanta have so dominated the tradition as to blot out these other expressions of *vedānta*. In many ways the tradition has, in effect, been frozen to the middle of the eighth century CE, yet we forget that these Upanishads belong to an age at least a thousand years before Shankara and even more prior to the times of Ramanuja and Madhva. So even Shankara Acharya comes quite late given the age of these Upanishads, yet such total dominance by Shankara and his followers has led to a stifling of newer and more modern forms of understanding and interpretation. Upanishadic scholarship tends to be stuck on the *vedānta* of eighth century India.

But from a modern perspective, we can legitimately ask why must there even be a *vedānta* in the first place? Why try to solve the inherent contradictions that exist within the Upanishads and the Bhagavad Gita or between the Shruti Vedas and the Smriti

Vedas? Why try to smooth out the tradition? The time differences between the two divisions of the Vedas alone are immense. Of course there are going to be differences and contradictions. Even the time differences between the various principal Upanishads span centuries. Of course there are going to be contradictions. Why must a religious tradition be perfectly uniform and consistent? Is it a matter of religious faith that drives this need to synthesize and smooth out a religious tradition—that if contradictions are found, they pose a challenge to religious faith and so must be resolved?

Perhaps modern comparative religion can help us resolve this problem and move on from eighth century India. One of the great accomplishments of modern comparative religion is the distinction that can be made between belief and faith. This was first brought to our attention by the theologian Wilford Cantwell Smith, who made this distinction back in the 1960s, in his book *The Meaning and End of Religion*. There he drew the distinction that within what we call religion are actually two components, an accumulated religious tradition and religious faith itself. The architecture, music, scriptures, doctrines, forms of dress, prayers, and even foods, etc., all form what he called the accumulated religious tradition. And then lying at the foundation of this accumulated tradition is the actual religious faith itself. The two interact: Faith produces the religious tradition in the first place and then in turn is nurtured and supported by that accumulated tradition.

If we accept this distinction, that belief and faith are not the same, then we realize that what one believes, the doctrines, the creeds, the theology, etc., are part of an accumulated tradition and therefore subject to change. Even the various forms of *vedānta* are part of this accumulated tradition. Of course beliefs will change over time as our understanding of the world changes. And yet a strong religious tradition is informed by its basic religious faith, which tends not to change. If we fail to see this distinction and think that religious faith and religious belief are the same, we force ourselves to become reactive and push ourselves into extreme positions of having to justify that faith when beliefs are challenged by changing circumstances. This often pushes us into anti-intellectual positions. A challenge to one's beliefs can easily create a crisis of faith; but when one understands the difference between belief and religious faith, then beliefs can change without affecting one's religious faith.

For a religious practitioner this is a liberating idea. One becomes freed from the need to rationalize or dismiss new circumstances. In the Western world probably the best example is Darwin's theory of evolution and how that was attacked when *Origin of Species* first appeared in 1859. Darwin was a direct challenge to the Christian beliefs of the day and therefore a challenge to Christian faith. Even today the attacks and denials still continue, particularly from Christian fundamentalism, which generally still fails to make the distinction between faith and belief.

Returning to the matter at hand, the Upanishads fall within the realm of scripture, part of the accumulated religious tradition of ancient India and therefore subject to change. Yet, they are sacred writings that have inspired faith and guided the lives of millions of human beings for millennia. The magic of scripture is its ability to inspire faith and recreate itself age after age and so reestablish its relevance from generation to generation. In this sense scripture is timeless. Why should these Upanishads be frozen to a certain time, the eighth century CE, and then only by one line of interpretation, Advaita Vedanta? Scripture belongs to the ages. I view the Upanishads as valuable and sacred works that also speak to our time and beyond India. They are the product of human theology as well as Hindu theology. They are relevant religious works that belong to the whole world as much as they belong to ancient India and Hinduism. Therefore, the present translation and annotations of these principal Upanishads have been largely made without recourse to any forms of *vedānta*, including Shankara's Advaita Vedanta. I wanted a fresh start. As the astronomer looks through a telescope and sees the light that has traveled for thousands of light years, similarly I wanted to look at the light of these Upanishads, see what they had to say in their time and then see what illumination they can provide us today, in our time and place, thousands of years since their inception.

Naturally, choosing to translate this way, consciously avoiding recourse to Indian traditions and commentators, creates certain limitation as well as advantages, and I am sure there will be criticism, particularly from devout Hindus who want to stay true to Hindu traditions. But there are hundreds of translations and studies that do precisely that. I direct my critics to them. This translation has been made by a Westerner who is also a practitioner. Given my Western perspective and knowing the distinction between faith and belief, I have tried to work with these sacred texts to find relevant meaning for who I am as a Westerner schooled in the West, but who is deeply involved in India and Hindu traditions. Being freed from the constraints of needing a *vedānta*, whether in the tradition of Shankara, Ramanuja or Madhva, allows me to look at these Upanishads in a new way.

What makes these Upanishads most valuable is their universal nature. They are generally non-sectarian and therefore outside of any particular religious tradition, even within India. They are not Vaishnavite, Shaivate, or part of the Shakta traditions. In general, no specific deity is mentioned as supreme. God remains unnamed. Of course, many deities and semi-divine beings are mentioned throughout the Upanishads. The sun, the moon, wind, rain are mentioned as deities. Many semi-divine beings, such as Gandharvas, are also mentioned. But when it comes to naming an ultimate being, God, no specific name is mentioned. Later Hindu traditions, which are sectarian in nature, glorify Vishnu, Shiva or Durga as that supreme Deity, but these principal Upanishads do not.

The main word for that Ultimate Source is *brahma,* and it is repeated over and over, but it is not the name of any specific deity. The word is neuter and is derived from the root *bṛh,* meaning to roar and expand. *Brahma* is ultimate power and force, and it is described as the substratum that underlies all existence and from which all things come and ultimately return. We also find words like *ātmā, puruṣa* and *īśa* being used to refer to that Supreme Source, but again they are not names. They are simply descriptions of that ultimate force and they respectively mean "supreme soul," "cosmic man" or "lord." Other such descriptive terms are also used, but never the name of a specific deity. This reluctance to impose the limitation of naming a specific deity is what gives the Upanishads their universal appeal. They are human yearnings for ultimate meaning and therefore a part of human religious thinking. Yes, they are part of the oldest Hindu traditions, but on a higher level they are not bound by geography and historical time, or even Hinduism itself. They are human and universal teachings.

These twelve principles Upanishads can be divided into three groups according to theme and historical development. The Brihad Aranyaka and the Chandogya Upanishads are what I call the sacrificial Upanishads. By "sacrificial" I mean Upanishads that focus on the Vedic *yajña* or *agni-hotra* fire ritual as their main emphasis. They are the oldest Upanishads. Next to them are the analytical Upanishads. These include the Taittiriya, Aitareya, Mandukya, Prashna, Mundaka, Kena, and the Katha Upanishads. By "analytical" I mean Upanishads that no longer build on the Vedic *yajña* as their theological foundation, but instead take an analytical approach in their teachings. The Taittiriya, for example, analyses the fire *kośas* or containers that make up our existence in this physical world, our food container (*anna-maya-kośa*), our breath container (*prāṇa-maya-kośa*) etc. The Mandukya Upanishad provides an analysis of four states of awareness, dream sleep, deep sleep, etc. The Mundaka Upanishad even criticizes Vedic ritual as inferior and just a distraction to the attainment of *brahma*. These analytical Upanishads appear after the sacrificial Upanishads. Later still are the Kaushitaki, Isha and the Shvetashvatara Upanishads, which are the devotional Upanishads as they offer prayers to that ultimate power *brahma* for salvation and protection in this world. They are the precursors of devotion (*bhakti*) best found in an even later work, the Bhagavad Gita, which is highly theistic in its devotion to Krishna.

There are a number themes running throughout the Upanishads that will be helpful in understanding these ancient works. The first is correspondence, that elements correspond to other elements. For example, the eye of God corresponds to the sun, which in turn corresponds to the eye of man. The breathing of God corresponds to the wind, which in turn corresponds to the breath within man. The mind of God corresponds to the moon, which in turn corresponds to the mind of man. The hairs on the body of God correspond to trees and vegetation, which in turn correspond to the hair on the body of man. Similar to this is the relationship between the macrocosm and the microcosm. The sun "up there" corresponds to a sun within man. The mars "up there" corresponds to a mars within man. In fact, this is the basis of Vedic astrology: Read the heavens "up there" and you can read the corresponding celestial bodies within man. The *ātmā* or soul of the cosmos corresponds to the soul within man. The *prāṇa* or life force of the cosmos is the life force within man. This theme of correspondence pervades the Shruti Vedas, and the Upanishads in particular.

Another related theme is the relationship between the whole and its parts. This famous verse from the Brihad Aranyaka (5.1.1) best captures this relationship:

pūrṇam ***adaḥ*** *pūrṇam* ***idam*** *pūrṇāt pūrṇam udacyate*
pūrṇasya pūrṇam ādāya pūrṇam evāvaśiṣyate

That is whole. **This** is whole. From wholeness, wholeness unfolds. Taking wholeness from wholeness, wholeness remains.

Here we see the use of two pronouns, *adas* and *idam*, "that" and "this." Looking out into the universe, the Upanishad says, "**That** is whole," the universe is whole. Then looking across this world, it says, "**This** is whole," this world is whole. Yet, in ordinary thinking we might say, yes, this universe is whole, but this world is just a part of that whole and therefore not whole. Yet here we are told that not only is the universe whole, the part is also whole! Then it goes on to say, take so many parts from this whole and still it remains whole! How can this be? If I have a whole pie and I take so many slices from that pie, the pie becomes smaller, incomplete. But here not only does the pie remain whole, the individual slices, the parts, are also whole. This implies that the whole is contained within the parts–that within every part of this world the whole is lying within. On another level the "that" refers to *brahma* (God) and the "this" refers to the individual *ātmā* or soul. Therefore, find the individual soul and you can find the universal soul. This is key to upanishadic thinking.

Another theme is *yajña*, sacrifice, particularly the fire sacrifice (*agni-hotra*). The two older Upanishads, the Brihad Aranyaka and the Chandogya, as we mentioned, especially focus on this ritual. In fact, the world is compared to an *agni-hotra*. The later primary Upanishads, the analytical upanishads move away from this theme and concentrate on less ritual matters of Hindu theology, but in this earliest period the *agni-hotra* is so important that it shapes the worldview of ancient Vedic culture. Simply put, the *agni-hotra* is about power. It was the overwhelming technology of the day. Creation took place with the help of the *agni-hotra*. This can clearly be seen in the opening chapters of both the Brihad Aranyaka and Chandogya Upanishads. The Brihad Aranyaka describes the world in terms of the horse sacrifice, the *aśva-medha-yajña*, which becomes a metaphor for the universe itself. The Chandogya Upanishad praises the power of sound and the mantras used in the *agni-hotra*. Both the gods and the demons use these rituals in the form of the High Chant, the *udgītha*, as they battle for control of the world.

The *agni-hotra* was an extremely elaborate and meticulous affair that was taken with absolute seriousness. In ancient times it was controlled by the priestly class, and it was so elaborate and costly that only the royal class and certain wealthy mercantile members had access to it. It conferred power, prestige and legitimacy on the royal order. Kings were coronated and given legitimacy by the priests using the *agni-hotra*. The fire sacrifice as we know it now is called a *havan* or *homa* depending on the region of India. It is still relevant and important in the daily lives of Hindus even as it has been democratized and made accessible to the common person. Today the *havan* or *homa* is a mere shadow of the *agni-hotra* as it was practiced in Vedic times. Hindu priests regularly perform these sacrifices in temples and the homes of Hindu families. Even though the fire sacrifice has been largely replaced by devotion it is still a significant part of Hindu religious life. In the days of the Upanishads, it was not just a part of the religious life—it **was** the religious life.

Another feature of the Upanishads is reductionism. What I mean by reductionism is the tendency to reduce life to its most basic level, the "nuts and bolts" of life, so to speak: breath, food, loneliness, power, etc. The Brihad Aranyaka and Chandogya Upanishads, for example, talks of food, breath, sex and power as the foundations of life. They even talk of loneliness as a reason for creation. God, *brahma*, felt alone and so, being alone and feeling the need for an other, creation burst forth. The very language of the Upanishads is simple and basic, yet sublime! Later Sanskrit texts like the Puranas have a much more embellished and flowery language involving complicated meters and word play, etc. The concepts and language of the Upanishads, however, are as simple and basic as language can be. And yet they are subtle and a delight to read!

There is a general understanding that the Upanishads only discuss the "high and mighty," which includes discussions of *brahma*, *ātmā* and *prāṇa,* God, the soul and life force. While this is certainly true, a lot more is discussed. A person who desires political power and progeny should perform the *agni-hotra* in a certain way. One who desires the destruction of enemies should also perform the *agni-hotra* according to certain rituals. A person who desires powerful sex should similarly perform the *agni-hotra*. One who desires the heavenly worlds wherein one can find unlimited pleasure can also follow the *agni-hotra* according to certain rituals.

The Upanishads are also full of geographic and historic references. Many times kings and priests come from various places to assemble for debate and wealth. The great King Janaka creates a contest wherein he entices the learned pundits of the day with the prize of cattle and gold. Yajnavalkya, the most learned scholar of his time, immediately comes and seizes the gold, to the horror of the other pundits. He boldly declares he is there for the gold. The Upanishads reflect human nature in all its forms, base and sublime. There are references to famine and drought and floods. There are references to social ideas involving caste, kings teaching *brāhmanas*, wealthy merchants and women receiving mystical knowledge, etc. There are references to female issues, including marriage, birth control and childbirth. There is misogyny. There is humor and satire. There is a section where priests are compared to chanting dogs barking for food and drink. And of course there is great poetry, and beautiful metaphors throughout. The honey talks from the Brihad Aranyaka Upanishad are exquisite.

These Upanishads show evidence of a religious shift. Joseph Campbell spoke of different religious types, namely religions of affirmation and religions of denial. Many early religions saw this world in positive terms. These are religions of affirmation and they tend to emphasize embracing and affirming the world as it is rather than seeking to escape it. An opposite religious mode is one of denial wherein the world is seen as blatantly evil, false and unreal. Such a religious view tends to focus on transcending or escaping the world of suffering and limitations. These religions often emphasize renunciation of worldly desires, ascetic practices, and detachment from material concerns. It is common within the same religious tradition to find these different phases of religious development at different times.

Within these principal Upanishads we can see evidence of religious affirmation in the earliest Upanishads with their emphasis on the Vedic sacrifice as a means to obtain whatever one desire in this world. Life was essentially good and the sacrifice was the means to contact the gods to obtain what was necessary to live happily. There was little concerns for salvation or release from this world. The Isha Upanishads tells us how to live a hundred years enjoying this world. It is a positive affirmation of life. But later on in the same principal Upanishads we can see a shift to a religion of denial. For example, the simple words *sat* and *asat* completely reverse their meaning from the early sacrificial Upanishads to the later devotional Upanishads thus suggesting a shift in religious type. The word *sat* literally means what is real and true. From *sat* we get the word *satya* which is generally translated as truth. *Asat* is the total opposite, what is unreal and untrue. In the later devotional Upanishads including works like the Bhagavad Gita, and throughout the *smriti* tradition, *sat* refers to God (*brahma*) and the soul (*ātmā*), whereas this physical world including the body are called *asat*, unreal and temporary. In other words, spiritual "things" are *sat* and physical "things" are *asat*. Yet in the early sacrificial Upanishads, especially the Brihad Aranyaka Upanishad *sat* is used to refer to this physical world while *asat* is used to refer to the unseen spiritual realm "up there" so to speak. And this makes good sense. This physical reality, what we see before us, **is** real. You can touch it, see it and walk on it. It is concrete and apparent, of course it is *sat*. On the other hand, the soul, God and a spiritual reality that may be "up there" or inside of us **is** unseen, intangible and elusive. It makes sense to call it *asat*. Referring to the world as *sat*, real and true, is an affirmation of the world. But the later shift to view the world as *asat*, unreal and false, is evidence of a religious shift from religious affirmation to religious denial. In its extreme form Advaita Vedanta uses the doctrine of illusion (*māyā*) to sees this world as false and something to become free from.

The Upanishads are therefore much more than simply theological documents. They are historical works, they are literature, and, most important of all, they are human documents. They arose within India and are the product of Hindu thought, yet they easily rise to the level of world theology, world literature, and world scripture.

1

Taittiriya Upanishad

Introduction to
Taittiriya Upanishad

The Taittiriya Upanishad includes verses that are prayers and benedictions, instructions on phonetics and pronunciation, advice on ethics and morals, along with philosophical instruction given to graduating students from ancient Vedic schools. It analyses the five *kośas* (bodies) or "containers" that make up our existence in this physical world, our food container (*anna-maya-kośa*), our breath container (*prāṇa-maya-kośa*), our mental container (*mano-maya-kośa*), our intellect container (*vijñāna-maya-kośa*), and our joy container (*ānanda-maya-kośa*).

The Taittiriya constitutes chapters seven, eight and nine of a much larger work, the Taittiriya Aranyaka, which is itself a supplement added to the Taittiriya Brahmana of the Black Yajur Veda. This Upanishad is classified as "black" because it is an "un-arranged" collection of verses from the Yajur Veda. This is in contrast to the "white" or well-arranged Yajur Veda where the Brihad Aranyaka Upanishad and Isha Upanishad are found.

The word *taittirīya* is obscure. A *taittira* is a bird like a partridge. Consequently, this Upanishad is said to be a collection of lessons obtained from mythical students who became "partridges" in order to gain knowledge. Alternatively, the word *taittirīya* means "from the sage Tittiri," who was a student of the ancient lexicographer Yaska.

The Taittiriya Upanishad has three chapters called *vallīs*: the *Śikṣha Vallī*, the *Ānanda Vallī* and the *Bhṛgu Vallī*. The *Śikṣha Vallī* includes twelve lessons called *anuvākas*. The *Ānanda Vallī* includes nine lessons, while the *Bhṛgu Valli* consists of ten lessons.

The date of Taittiriya Upanishad, along with the other Vedic era literature, is unclear. However, there is enough evidence to suggest that the Taittiriya Upanishad is one of the early Upanishads, likely composed in the first half of the first millennium BCE, after the Brihad Aranyaka and the Chandogya Upanishads. It is therefore pre-Buddhist in origin.

Śikṣāvallī Vallī

(First Section)

First *Anuvāka*

Invocation

May Mitra, Varuna, and Aryaman be good to us!
May Indra, Brihaspati, and the expansive Vishnu be good to us!
Respects to *brahma*. Respects to you, O Vayu, for you are the visible *brahma.*
I will speak of you as the visible *brahma.*
I will speak of what is right and of what is true.
Let this benefit me.
Let this benefit the speaker.
Indeed, let this benefit both the student and the teacher.
Peace to all. Peace to all.

Second *Anuvāka*

Aspects of Pronunciation

1. *Om*! We will now speak of pronunciation: letters, tone, vowel length and strength, articulation and combination. These are the aspects of pronunciation.

Third *Anuvāka*

The Divisions of Sacred Learning

1–3. May we attain fame!
May we attain the splendor of sacred learning!

I will now explain this sacred learning with all its divisions. There are five divisions to be discussed:

In relation to the worlds,
In relation to light,
In relation to knowledge,
In relation to progeny, and
In relation to the body.

Now, as it relates to the worlds: On the one hand, there is the earth; on the other hand, there are the heavens. Sky is the in-between, and wind is the link. This is with reference to the worlds.

Now, as it relates to light: On the one hand, there is fire; on the other hand, there is the sun. Water is the in-between, and lightning is the link. This is with reference to light.

Now, as it relates to knowledge: On the one hand, there is a teacher; on the other hand, there is a student. Learning is the in-between, and instruction is the link. This is with reference to knowledge.

Now, as it relates to progeny: On the one hand, there is mother; on the other hand, there is father. Offspring are the in-between,

---

[1] The sound "*Om*."

[2] The word is *indra*. It could also be translated as the god Indra.

[3] *Svāhā* is a word uttered after an oblation has been made into a sacrificial fire. These are, therefore, prayers meant to be recited during a sacrificial fire offering.

and procreation is the link. This is with reference to progeny.

4. Now, as it relates to the body: On the one hand, there is the lower jaw; on the other hand, there is the upper jaw. Speech is the in-between, and the tongue is the link. This is with reference to the body.

This is a breakdown of the major divisions. One who understands this obtains offspring, livestock, the splendor of sacred knowledge, food, and the heavenly worlds.

Fourth *Anuvāka*

A Teacher's Prayer

1-2. May that bull[1] of the Vedas, who assumes all forms, who has sprung from the immortal hymns of the Vedas, may that king[2] bestow wisdom upon me. O God, may I attain immortality.

May my body become strong.
May my tongue be sweet.
May my ears hear only what is true.
You are the abode of *brahma*.
Protected by wisdom,
Guard what I have learned.

She brings wealth. She spreads wealth. She creates wealth for herself and for me. Accompanied with garments and cows, food and drink, let her bring opulence. Without delay bring sheep and cattle! *Svāhā.*[3]

May students seek me. *Svāhā.*
May students find me. *Svāhā.*
May students rush to me. *Svāhā.*
May they have discipline. *Svāhā.*
May they attain peace. *Svāhā.*

3. May I become famous. *Svāhā.*
May I find wealth. *Svāhā.*
Enter me, O Wealth,
And may I enter you. *Svāhā.*
You are a river, many-branched;
O Wealth, cleanse me. *Svāhā.*

As water flows down a slope,
As the months turn into years,
O Creator, may students come to me. *Svāhā.*

You are my neighbor.
Shine on me.
Enter me!

---

[4] The word *vyāhṛti* is literally an utterance. Here *vyāhṛti* is translated as a "call" because it is an utterance that is repeatedly called out during a fire sacrifice.

[5] The four calls are divided four ways: according to the worlds, according to lights, according to Vedic recitations, and according to breaths, thus giving rise to four sets of four with their respective correspondences.

Fifth *Anuvāka*

The Four Calls

1-2 There are three special "calls":[4] *bhūr*, *bhuvas,* and *suvar.* Now, according to the son of Mahacamasa, a fourth call should be added, namely, *mahas*. *Mahas* is *brahma*. It is like the body while the other deities are limbs.

Bhūr is the world. *Bhuvas* is the sky. *Suvar* is the world beyond. *Mahas* is the sun. In the sun all these worlds experience joy.

Then again:

Bhūr is fire. *Bhuvas* is wind. *Suvar* is the sun. *Mahas* is the moon. In the moon all these luminaries experience joy.

Bhūr is the Rig. *Bhuvas* is the Sama. *Suvar* is the Yajur. *Mahas* is *brahma*. In *brahma* all these Vedas experience joy.

Bhūr is the incoming breath. *Bhuvas* is the outgoing breath. *Suvar* is the held breath. *Mahas* is food. In food all these breaths experience joy.

In this way these four calls are understood in four ways, making four sets of four calls.[5] One who knows this knows *brahma.* May the gods pay tribute to such a person.

Sixth *Anuvāka*

The Ancient Path of Yoga

1-2. There is a space within the heart where a person, consisting of mind and who is immortal and luminous, resides. From that space Indra's passage travels through a place between the soft and hard palate where that nipple-like flesh hangs down.[6] It ends at the crown of the skull where the hair parts.[7] This person travels along this passage and first establishes himself in fire with the call *bhūr*, then in wind with the call *bhuvas*, then in the sun with the call *suvar*, and finally in *brahma* with the call *mahas*. In this way he obtains complete freedom and self-mastery and becomes the lord of the mind, speech, sight, hearing, and understanding. He becomes like *brahma*, whose body is space, whose *ātmā* is truth, whose pleasure is breath, and whose joy is mind. Thus he is tranquil and immortal. This is the ancient path of the *yogīs*. Proceed in this way.

[6] This is a reference to the palatine uvula, which is the nipple like projection that hangs down from the back edge of the soft palate between the tonsils.

[7] This is a reference to the *suṣumnā nāḍī* of Patanjali's yoga system. This is a pathway which passes from the heart upward through the middle region of the throat at the point of the uvula, and then up to the skull where the hair parts. This is said to be the birthplace of Indra, hence the name *indra-yoni.*

Seventh *Anuvāka*

The Essential Elements

1. The essential elements of the world are earth, sky, the heavens, the directions, and the intermediate directions; fire, wind, sun, moon and stars in another group; and water, herbs, trees, space and the body in a final group.

The essential elements of the body are the five breaths, sight, hearing, mind, speech, touch, skin, flesh, sinew, bone and marrow.

Considering all this, a sage has declared, "The world is fivefold. By means of the fivefold one secures the fivefold."

Eighth *Anuvāka*

The Uses of *Om*

Om is *brahma*. All this is *om*. *Om* is agreement. When asked to recite, they first say *om*, then they recite. They utter *om* before singing the *sama* hymns. They utter *om śom* before they recite the sacred texts. Beginning with *om*, the *adhvaryu* priest utters the response chant. Beginning with *om*, the *brahmā* priest utters the introductory praise. One says *om* before giving permission to perform the sacred fire ritual. Before making a sacred invocation, a *brāhmana* will utter *om*. When one wishes to obtain the Vedas he first utters *om*. As he receives the Vedas he says *om*.

Ninth *Anuvāka*

Study and Teaching of the Vedas

1. Sacred tradition, yes, but only along with study and teaching of the Vedas.
Truth, yes, but only along with study and teaching of the Vedas.
Austerity, yes, but only along with study and teaching of the Vedas.
Self discipline, yes, but only along with study and teaching of the Vedas.
Peacefulness, yes, but only along with study and teaching of the Vedas.
Maintaining the sacred fires, yes, but only along with study and teaching of the Vedas.
The Agni Hotra, yes, but only along with study and teaching of the Vedas.
Caring for guests, yes, but only along with study and teaching of the Vedas.
Humaneness, yes, but only along with study and teaching of the Vedas.
Offspring, yes, but only along with study and teaching of the Vedas.
Procreation, yes, but only along with study and teaching of the Vedas.
Descendants, yes, but only along with study and teaching of the Vedas.

"Just the truth"—that was the view of Rathitara
the Truthful.
"Just austerity"—that was the view of Pauru-
shishti the Ever-Austere.

"Nothing but study and teaching of the Vedas"—that was the view of Maudgalya the Painless; for that is austerity. Indeed, that is austerity.

Tenth *Anuvāka*

Trisanku's Prayer

I am the shaker of the tree.
My fame rises upward like a mountain.
High and pure, bestowing strength and power,
I am the brightest treasure. I am shining wisdom,
Immortal and without decay.
This is the prayer of Trisanku.

Eleventh *Anuvāka*

Graduation Instructions

1. After graduation the teacher instructs his students. Parting instructions: Always speak the truth. Practice *dharma*. Do not neglect to study. Pay your teacher properly, and then do not cut off relations with him or your family of students. Do not neglect truth. Do not neglect *dharma*. Do not neglect your personal health. Do not neglect your wealth. Do not neglect to study and teach.

2. Do not neglect the rites to the gods and the ancestors. Treat your mother as a god. Treat your father as a god. Treat your teacher as a god. Treat a guest as a god. Only those actions that are blameless are to be performed, and not others. Those good deeds you have seen us perform, you should also perform, and not others.

3-4. You should honor learned people with a seat. Give with faith, never without faith. Give with grace. Give with modesty. Give with caution. Give with understanding. And if an action or rite is to be performed, and some learned and gentle people who are devoted to the law are present, consult them as to what is right and what is wrong. As they do, you should do. In matters of controversy, if some learned and gentle people who are devoted to the law are present, consult them as to what is right and what is wrong. As they do, you should do. This is the command. This is the instruction. This is the hidden teaching of the Vedas. This is the lesson. This wisdom should be venerated. Indeed, this wisdom should be venerated.

---

[8] This last chapter is identical with the first chapter of this section except the tense has changed.

Twelfth *Anuvāka*

Concluding Benediction[8]

May Mitra, Varuna, and Aryaman be good to us!
May Indra, Brihaspati, and the expansive Viṣṇu be good to us!
Respects to *brahma*. Respects to you, O Vayu, for you are the visible *brahma.*
I have spoken of you alone as the visible *brahma.*
I have spoken of what is right and of what is true.
It has benefited me.
It has benefited the speaker.
Indeed, it has benefited both the student and the teacher.
Peace to all. Peace to all.

Here ends the first *Vallī,* entitled *Śikṣāvallī*

[1] This is a famous invocation that repeats at the beginning of the third *vallī*. Even though this invocation is famous, not all editions include it.

[2] Other than the pronoun, there is no stated subject in this invocation. Consequently, some translators take God as the subject: "May God help both of us." Others take study itself as the subject: "May this study help both of us."

[3] The word is *ākāśa*, which is generally rendered as "space," and by space we mean the gap between two points.

Ānanda-Vallī
(Second Section)
First *Anuvāka*

Invocation[1]

Om
May this[2] help us.
May this nourish us.
May this make us strong.
May our study fill us with light.
May we ever remain friends.
Om
May all find peace!

The knower of *brahma* attains the supreme, for it has been said:

Brahma is truth. *Brahma* is knowledge.
Brahma is eternal. *Brahma* resides in the most secret place.
Brahma is in the highest realm.
The one who knows this fulfills all his desires.
Such a person is all-knowing like *brahma*.

From *brahma* space[3] has come. From space the wind blows. From the wind fire burns. From fire waters flow. From waters earth appears. From the earth all plants appear. From plants food arises and from food mankind appears, for food is the essence of mankind. Here is his head. Here is his right wing. Here is his left wing. This is his upper torso, and here is his tail, which is his foundation.[4] In this regard there is the following verse:

Second *Anuvāka*

Food[5]

All beings are born from food.
On food they live and into food they return.
Food is foremost among beings.
For this reason food is called the source of all.[6]

---

[4] Here a man is compared to a bird. Interestingly, the Vedic fire sacrifice is also compared to an eagle or hawk. The fire container is often built to resemble a falcon.

[5] This is the beginning of a section which describes five different bodies that are "nested" inside of each other: the food-body, the breath-body, the mind-body, the intellect-body, and the joy-body. Sometimes they are called sheaths (*kośa*). So they are called respectively *anna-maya-kośa*,the sheath made of food; *prāna-maya-kośa*, the sheath made of breath; *mano-maya-kośa*, the sheath made of mind; *vijñāna-maya-kośa*, the sheath made of intellect, and *ānanda-maya-kośa*, the sheath made of joy. This is also a progression from coarse to subtle. It also corresponds to different realizations of divinity. The lowest level is where one sees life in terms of the basic necessities, symbolized by food. The highest level is the aesthetic level, where one sees beauty (*rasa*) as the highest expression of divinity.

[6] The word is *sarvauṣadha,* which is literally "made of grass."

[7] The word for food is *anna*. It is derived from the root *ad*, to eat. All creatures eat food, yet those same creatures, being made of food, are eaten by food. Hence the idea that food is eaten and food eats.

Those who recognize food as *brahma* obtain food.

Food is foremost among beings.
For this reason food is called the source of all.
Beings are born from food. Beings are sustained by food.
Food is eaten by beings. Food eats beings.
For this reason it is called *anna.*[7]

But different from and lying within this food-body is another body consisting of *prāṇa*, which completely fills and pervades a man. This breath-body follows the form of a man and so has the appearance of a man. The in-breath is the head of this body. Its right side is the held-breath and its left side is the out-breath. Space is its soul, and earth is its tail and foundation. In this regard there is the following verse:

Third *Anuvāka*
Breath

Gods, men and animals all breathe to obtain *prāṇa*,
for *prāṇa* is the life of beings.
Therefore, it is called all-life. Those who venerate
prāṇa as *brahma* surely have a full life,
for *prāṇa* is the life of beings. For this reason it is
called all-life.

This breath-body indeed is the inner essence of the food-body.

But different from and lying within this breath-body is another body, consisting of mind, which completely fills and pervades a man. This mind-body follows the form of a man and so has the appearance of a man. The Yajur Veda is the head of this body. Its right side is the Rig Veda and its left side is the Sama Veda. Instruction is its soul, and the Atharva and Angirasa hymns are its tail and foundation. In this regard there is the following verse:

Fourth *Anuvāka*
Mind

That person who has experienced the joy of knowing *brahma*, which is beyond the reach of the mind and words, becomes free of fear.

This mind-body indeed is the inner essence of the breath-body.

But different from and lying within that mind-body is another body, consisting of intellect.[8] It completely fills and pervades a man. This intellect-body follows the form of a man and so has the appearance of a man. Faith is the head of this body. Its right

[8] The word is *vijñāna,* which could also be rendered as knowledge, wisdom, or even perception.

[9] *Rita* here has been rendered as sacred tradition, but it could also be translated as divine law, what is proper, what is right, etc.

[10] The word here is *mahat*, which is literally "the Great." In *Sānkhya* philosophy the *mahat* refers to the *pradhāna,* which is the source of the material world. We might describe this as the mass of energy out of which this material world flows.

side is sacred tradition[9] and its left side is truth. Yoga is its soul, and the Great[10] is its tail and foundation. In this regard there is the following verse:

Fifth *Anuvāka*
Intellect

Intellect directs the sacrifice. Intellect performs the rites.
And so all the gods venerate intellect as the highest *brahma.*
If one recognizes intellect as *brahma*, and if one never deviates from this understanding, leaving all evils in the body, he enjoys all his desires.

This intellect-body indeed is the inner essence of the mind-body.

But different from and lying within that intellect-body is another body, consisting of joy. It completely fills and pervades a man. This joy-body follows the form of a man and so has the appearance of a man. Pleasure is the head of this body. Its right side is delight and its left side is thrill. Joy is its soul, and *brahma* itself is its tail and foundation. In this regard there is the following verse:

Sixth *Anuvāka*
Joy

If one thinks *brahma* is nonexistent,
One becomes nonexistent.
If one thinks *brahma* is existent,
Then people know that person to be existent.

This joy-body indeed is the inner essence of the intellect-body.

But a question arises:

> Can a person who lacks knowledge of *brahma* go to that yonder world upon leaving this world? Or does only the person who has knowledge of *brahma* go there?[11]

He had this desire: I should become many. Let me produce offspring. He did penance. Having performed penance, he created

---

[11] If *brahma* is so pervasive and so real, then why does only the man of knowledge achieve it? Why not the ignorant as well? The question is asked, but not answered.

[12] *Sukṛta,* literally "well done." Here the teaching is saying that creation is good, well done. Throughout the Upanishads and earlier Vedas we see creation described using words that are positive. We have many times seen the word *sat* used to describe creation. *Sat* means what is real, good, and pure. Now we will see the word *rasa* used, which means juice and taste and essence. All of these are positive affirmations for the nature of creation. The Vedantic notion that the world was illusory (*māyā*), unreal (*asat*), false (*anṛta*), and full of suffering (*duḥkha*) is a later idea. In its earliest form the nature of reality was seen in positive terms: The world was to be embraced, enjoyed, and engaged.

[13] The word *rasa* means juice, taste, or essence. Throughout this section the two words *rasa* and *ānanda* are positive perceptions of reality. The idea is that the highest appreciation of reality is in terms of aesthetics, the appreciation of the divine in terms of play and joy.

[14] The words are *udaram antaram,* which is literally a "bulge within."

all this world. Having created it, he entered into it; and having entered into it, it became this real *(sat)* world and that yonder (*tyat*) world, the distinct and the indistinct, the supported and the unsupported, the perceived and the unperceived, the true and the false. He became all things, whatever there is. That is why people call all this *sat,* the Real. In this regard there is the following verse:

Seventh *Anuvāka*

Rasa

In the beginning there was only *asat,*
And from *asat sat* was born
It created a body for itself.
For this reason it is called well made.[12]

That ultimate reality which is well made is verily *rasa;*[13] and when it is grasped, it is the cause of supreme joy. If this joy did not exist in all places, who would breath in, who would breath out? This *rasa* indeed is the cause of supreme joy. When a person is grounded in that reality which is unseen, bodiless, undefined, and without support, he becomes fearless. But when one creates differentiation[14] in this reality, it leads to fear. This is the fear of one who does not understand.

On this there is the following verse:

Eighth *Anuvāka*

Happiness

In fear of *brahma* the wind blows.
In fear of *brahma* the sun rises.
In fear of *brahma* fire burns and Indra creates rain.
In fear of *brahma* death rushes towards all.

Now an analysis of happiness.

Assume a youth who is good, learned, quick, handsome and strong. He possesses all the wealth of the earth. This is one measure of human happiness.[15]

Now consider a hundred such measures of human happiness. This is the happiness of terrestrial Gandharvas and a man who is learned in the Vedas and who is free of desire.[16]

Now consider a hundred such measures of terrestrial Gandharvas' happiness. This is the happiness of celestial Gandharvas and a man who is learned in the Vedas and who is free of desire.

---

[15] An analysis of the range of happiness will be described. The highest level of human happiness becomes the standard measure of happiness by which we understand the increasing degrees of happiness for higher beings.

[16] The person of learning has the highest degree of happiness. That is why this sentence is repeated throughout.

Now consider a hundred such measures of celestial Gandharvas' happiness. This is the happiness of the ancestors who dwell in their heavenly worlds and a man who is learned in the Vedas and who is free of desire.

Now consider a hundred such measures of ancestors' happiness. This is the happiness of the terrestrial gods and a man who is learned in the Vedas and who is free of desire.

Now consider a hundred such measures of terrestrial gods' happiness. This is the happiness of the gods who have attained their position through good works and a man who is learned in the Vedas and who is free of desire.

Now consider a hundred such measures of happiness of the gods who have attained their position through good works. This is the happiness of the celestial gods and a man who is learned in the Vedas and who is free of desire.

Now consider a hundred such measures of celestial gods' happiness. This is the happiness of Indra and a man who is learned in the Vedas and who is free of desire.

Now consider a hundred such measures of Indra's happiness. This is the happiness of Brihaspati and a man who is learned in the Vedas and who is free of desire.

Now consider a hundred such measures of Brihaspati's happiness. This is the happiness of Prajapati and a man who is learned in the Vedas and who is free of desire.

Now consider a hundred such measures of Prajapati's happiness. This is the happiness of *brahma*[17] and a man who is learned in the Vedas and who is free of desire.

This one who exists within a man and that one who exists within the sun are one and the same. Understanding this, upon leaving this world this man first goes to the food-body, then the breath-body, then the mind-body, then the intellect-body, and finally into the joy-body.

In this regard there is the following verse.

Ninth *Anuvāka*

Conclusion

That person who knows the joy of *brahma*,
which is beyond the reach of words and the mind,
is free of fear.[18]

Such a person is never tormented by the thoughts "Why did I not do the right thing? Why did I do bad?" The person who knows *brahma* frees himself from these two thoughts. Indeed, he is freed from such duality!

Here ends this sacred teaching.

Here Ends the Second *Vallī* entitled *Ānanda-Vallī*

---

[17] Some translators render this as the creator god, Brahmā instead of *brahma*. They are taking the word as masculine instead of neuter.

[18] This is a close repetition of the opening verse in the fourth *Anuvāka*.

Bhṛgu-vallī

(Third Section)

First *Anuvāka*

Om

May this[1] help us.
May this nourish us.
May this make us strong.
May our study fill us with light.
May we ever remain friends.
May all find peace!

1. Bhrigu, the son of Varuna, once approached his father and said, "Sir, teach me about *brahma.*" His father instructed him about *brahma* as food and breath, sight and hearing, and as mind and speech. His father further said, "That from which all beings are born, that by which they are sustained, and that to which they enter upon death, that you should try to know. It is *brahma.*" Bhrigu then went to practice austerities and to reflect on these teachings. He soon returned and observed:

2. "*Brahma* is food! For it is from food that beings are born. It is from food they live, and it is to food they return at death." Having realized this, he returned to his father and spoke: "Sir, teach me about *brahma.*" So his father spoke: "Through austerities try to understand *brahma*. For *brahma* is austerity!" He went away and practiced austerities. Then he returned and observed:

3. "*Brahma* is breath! For it is from breath that all beings are born. It is from breath they live, and it is to breath they return at death." Having realized this, he returned to his father and once again spoke. "Sir, teach me about *brahma.*" So his father spoke: "Through austerities try to understand *brahma*. For *brahma* is austerity!" He went away and practiced austerities. Then he returned and observed:

4. "*Brahma* is mind! For it is out of mind that all beings are born. It is with mind they live, and it is to mind they return at the time of death." Having realized this, he returned to his father and once again spoke: "Sir, teach me about *brahma.*" So his father spoke: "Through austerities try to understand *brahma*. For *brahma* is austerity!" He went away and practiced austerities. Then he returned and observed:

5. "*Brahma* is intellect! For it is out of intellect all beings are born. It is with intellect they live, and it is to intellect they return at death." Having realized this, he returned to his father once again and spoke. "Sir, teach me about *brahma.*" So his father spoke: "Through austerities try to understand *brahma*. For *brahma* is austerity!" He went away and practiced austerities.

---

[1] There is no stated subject anywhere in this invocation. Some translators say God, "May God help both of us." Others say "study" is the subject.

[2] For example, digestion.

[3] For example, in a rain cloud.

[4] For example, during perspiration.

Then he returned and observed:

6. "*Brahma* is joy! For it is out of joy that all beings are born. It is with joy they live, and it is to joy they return at death." This is the teaching of Bhrigu, son of Varuna. This teaching is fixed in heaven, and so the one who knows this also becomes fixed. Such a person possesses food and eats food. He becomes great with offspring, livestock, sacred learning and fame.

7. One should not belittle food. That is the rule. Breath and food are the same. The body eats food. The body is founded on breath, and breath is founded on the body. Thus, food is founded on food. When a person knows that food is built on food, he becomes fixed. Such a person possesses food and eats food. He becomes great with offspring, livestock, sacred learning and fame.

8. One should not overlook food. That is the rule. Water and food are the same. Fire eats food,[2] and fire is found in water.[3] Water is found in fire.[4] Therefore, food is found in food. When someone knows that food is found in food, he becomes fixed. Such a person possesses food and eats food. He becomes great with offspring, livestock, sacred learning and fame.

9. One should prepare a lot of food. That is the rule. The earth and food are the same. Space eats food. Space is founded on the earth. The earth is founded on space. Therefore, food is founded on food. When a person knows that food is built on food, he becomes fixed. Such a person possesses food and eats food. He

becomes great with offspring, livestock, sacred learning and fame.

10.1. A guest should never be turned away from one's home. That is the rule. By every means one should prepare a lot of food. In this way they say, "Food is always available from him." When food is prepared at the beginning, it is available from him at the beginning. When food is prepared at the middle, it is available from him at the middle. When food is prepared at the end, it is available from him at the end.[5]

10.2-3. This is the way for one who knows this. In human terms, one sees *brahma* as peace in speech, one sees *brahma* as preservation in the incoming and outgoing breath, one sees *brahma* as action in the hands, one sees *brahma* as movement in the feet,

[5] The precise meanings of the expressions that I have translated as "at the beginning... at the middle... and at the end" (*mukhata*, *madhyata*, and *antata*) are unclear. They may refer to the times of a person's life (youth, middle age, and old age) or to the time of day when food is prepared for guests (morning, midday, and evening).

[6] Here the word is *brahma*, so the literal translation would be "Let him see that as *brahma* and he will possess *brahma*." The word *brahma* has many levels of meaning and so the translations can vary widely. One might render it "Let him see *that* as the supreme and he will possess the supreme." Another translator renders it "Let him see that as a magic formula and he will possess a magic formula." Another might be "Let him see that as the Vedas and he will possess the Vedas."

and one sees *brahma* as evacuation in the anus. In godly terms, one sees *brahma* as satisfaction in the rains, one sees *brahma* as power in lightning, one sees *brahma* as fame in livestock, one sees *brahma* as light in the luminaries, one sees *brahma* as procreation, immortality and joy in the sexual organ, and one sees *brahma* as totality in space.

Let him see *brahma* as the foundation and he will possess a foundation. Let him see *brahma* as might and he will have might. Let him see *brahma* as the mind and he will have a powerful mind.

10.4-5. Let him see *brahma* in bowing down; then all his desires will bow down to him. Let him see *brahma* as truth[6] and he will possess truth. Let him see *brahma* as an all-destructive power and his hated enemies and adversaries will perish.

This one here in man is the same as that one there in the sun. A man who knows this, when he passes from this world, first departs the body made of food, then the body made of breath, then the body made of mind, then the body made of intellect, and finally the body made of joy. He then travels throughout these worlds eating whatever he likes and taking whatever form he desires while singing the following chant:

O joy! O joy! O joy!
I am food! I am food! I am food!
I am a food eater! I am a food eater! I am a food eater!
I am the maker of fame. I am the maker of fame. I am the maker of fame.
I am the first born of truth,
Born before the gods.
I am at the center of immortality.
The one who gives me is the one who sustains me!

I am food!
I eat the food eater!
I have overcome this world!
I am the light of the world!

And so too for anyone who knows these secret teachings!

Here ends the *Bhrigu Vallī*
Here ends this Taittiriya Upanishad

2

Aitareya Upanishad

Introduction to

Aitareya Upanishad

The Aitareya Upanishad is part of the Rig Veda and is one of the primary Upanishads. It is divided into three chapters that deal with the creation of the world.

Chapter One: The Creation of the world
This chapter begins with the creation of the world, emphasizing that everything originated from the *ātmā*. It describes the creation of various elements of the world and the birth of human consciousness.

Chapter Two: The Three Births
This chapter delves into the concept of three births. In summary, the first birth takes place when a man injects semen into a woman. The second birth takes place when the child, who is the father in another form, is born from the mother's womb. The third birth is the father's rebirth.

Chapter Three: The Nature of Consciousness
The final chapter explores the nature of consciousness, describing how the *ātmā* manifests as both universal and individual consciousness. It explains how consciousness is responsible for the perception of the world and emphasizes the unity of all beings, underlining the idea that *ātmā* and *brahma* are the same.

First *Khaṇḍa*
First *Adhyāya*
Creation

1. In the beginning *ātmā* alone existed.[1] No other eyes looked on. It looked out and thought, "Let me create worlds."

2. It created the waters in heaven,[2] the lights in the sky,[3] the mortals, and the waters of the earth. The waters in heaven are beyond the sky, and so the sky itself is its foundation. The lights are the stars in heaven. The earth is the realm of death, and that which is underneath are the waters of the earth.

3. Seeing all this, *ātmā* thought, "Now I should create guardians[4] for these worlds." And so it drew forth from the waters of the earth a man who was without form. It gave him form.

---

[1] The earliest creation myth from the Rig Veda (10.129) begins "In the beginning there was neither *asat* nor *sat,* non-being nor being." The first Upanishad creation myth (BU 1.2) begins "In the beginning there was *sat* alone"; a later version (CU 3.1) says, "In the beginning there was *asat* alone." Here, an even later version, we are getting a story which says, "In the beginning there was *ātmā*." We are progressively moving from abstract to something more concrete.

[2] *Ambha*, clouds.

[3] The word is *marīci*, which is literally a ray of light or a spark of fire.

[4] The expression is *loka-pālān*, protectors of the world.

4. *Ātmā* nurtured this man. Like an egg, it fashioned a mouth. From that mouth sprang speech, and from speech came fire. It fashioned a nose, and from the nose sprang the in-breath,[5] and from the in-breath came the wind. It fashioned eyes, and from the eyes sprang sight, and from sight came the sun. It fashioned ears, and from the ears sprang hearing, and from hearing came the directions. It fashioned skin, and from the skin sprang hairs, and from the hairs came plants and trees. It fashioned a heart, and from the heart sprang the mind, and from the mind came the moon. It fashioned a navel, and from the navel sprang the down-breath, and from that down-breath came death.[6] Finally, it fashioned a penis, and from the penis sprang semen, and from semen came waters.

---

[5] *Prāṇa*, one of the five breaths or "winds" of the body.

[6] The body has five breaths or winds. Here the named wind is the *apāna*. This is the elimination system. Hence its connection with death.

[7] Here the different organs of the body that have been fashioned out of this shapeless man are referred to as divinities, *devatās*. The word *devatā* comes from the root d*iv,* which means to shine. Thus the organs of the body are "shining ones."

[8] This "vast ocean" is the water below the earth. It is a metaphor for *samsāra,* the cycle of birth and death.

Second *Khaṇḍa*
Creation Continued

1-3. Having been created, these divinities[7] fell into a vast ocean,[8] wherein they were afflicted by hunger and thirst. They spoke to *ātmā:* "Find us a place where we can live and eat." *Ātmā* brought them a cow. But they said, "This is not sufficient for us!" *Ātmā* brought them a horse. Again they said, "This too is not sufficient!" *Ātmā* brought them a man, and they said, "Well done! Indeed, a man is well made!"

Ātmā then told them, "Enter into your respective places!"

4. Fire became speech and entered the mouth; wind became breath and entered the nostrils; the sun became sight and entered the eye; the directions became hearing and entered the ears; plants and trees became bodily hair and entered the skin; the moon became mind and entered the heart; death became the down-breath and entered the navel; and waters became semen and entered the penis.

5. Hunger and thirst then spoke: "Find us a place too!"

Ātmā spoke to them: "I give you a portion of what belongs to all these divinities; I make you a partner with them. Therefore, to whatever deity one may make an offering, hunger and thirst share it with that divinity."

Third *Khaṇḍa*

Food

1. Ātmā then thought, "Now that these worlds and their guardians have been created, let me create food for them."

2-9. So it heated the waters, and from those waters something solid arose. It became food. No sooner had it been created than food began to flee.[9] *Ātmā* immediately tried to catch it with speech, but could not. For had food been caught by speech, then just by speaking about food one would be satisfied. *Ātmā* tried to catch it with breath, but could not. For had food been caught by breath, then just by breathing on food one would be satisfied.

---

[9] That which is to be eaten runs away from its eater.

[10] The breath which catches food is *apāna,* the breath of digestion.

[11] Here the wind is called *annāyu*, living by food. This again is the digestive system, which has previously been said to be a place of death.

[12] A body, with all its organs and other parts is like a well assembled house. But without a person to dwell within it, that house is useless. So the *ātmā* considered how to enter that house.

[13] The body is said to have eleven doorways: the sagittal suture, that soft spot that one feels on a young child before the skull fuses together; two eyes, two ears, two nostrils, the mouth, the navel, the penis, and the anus. The *ātmā* is said to enter and leave the body through this split between the two parts of the skull, the sagittal suture.

Ātmā tried to catch it with sight, but could not. For had food been caught by sight, then just by seeing food one would be satisfied. *Ātmā* tried to catch it with hearing, but could not. For had food been caught by hearing, then just by hearing about food one would be satisfied. *Ātmā* tried to catch it with touch, but could not. For had it been caught by touch, then just by feeling food one would be satisfied. *Ātmā* tried to catch it with mind, but could not. For had it been caught by mind, then just by thinking about food one would be satisfied. *Ātmā* tried to catch it with the penis, but could not. For had it been caught by the penis, then just by ejaculating one's hunger would be satisfied.

10. Finally, the down-breath[10] tried to catch this food. Food was caught. And so it is the wind that catches food. Wind indeed is the finder of food.[11]

11. Then it thought, "How can food survive without me? By what means can I enter it? If speaking is done through speech, if breathing is done through the breath, if seeing is done through the eye, if hearing is done through the ear, if touching is done through the skin, if thinking is done through the mind, if the in-breath is for breathing, and if procreation is done through the penis, then who am I?"[12]

12. So it split the skull at the parting of the hair and entered through that door. This door is called *vidṛti,* and it is a place of great joy.[13] This *ātmā* within the body has three dwelling places, three states of sleep as it were. This is one place, that is another

place, and this is still another place.[14]

13. Having taken birth, *ātmā* looked out upon all these beings and thought, "What more can anyone say?" For *ātmā* saw in this creation the cosmic person, the all-pervading *brahma,* and

---

[14] The reference is obscure. Commentators suggest these three places are the waking state, the dream state, and deep sleep. Another explanation is that the right eye is the abode during the waking state, the inner mind during dream state, and the space of the heart during deep sleep. Another explanation is the body of one's father, the body of the mother, and then one's own body. Sayana, commentator on the Vedas, suggests these three places are the right eye, the throat, and the heart.

[15] The expression is *idam ādarśam iti,* "this I have seen." The "this" referred to here I am taking as both the creation and man. It shows the relationship between the cosmic body and the individual body.

[16] The word *idandra* is a combination of *idam*, "this," and *dṛś,* "to see." Thus it has the same meaning as *idam adarsanam*. See fn above.

[17] See BU 4.2.2 and BU 3.4.1

[18] According to this Upanishad, it is man who owns the embryo.

[19] The new body is, of course, his son or daughter. Again, this whole section implies not only that the man has ownership over the fetus, but also ownership over the offspring, particularly a son. In fact, the father is the son.

[20] The words are *puṇya karma,* which can be understood as ritual actions meant to create merit for the attainment of heaven, or simply good deeds to benefit the world. The former is probably the intended meaning.

[21] In summary, the first birth takes place when a man injects semen into a woman. The second birth takes place when the child, who is the father in another form, is born from the mother's womb. The third birth is the father's rebirth.

declared, "This I have seen. Indeed, this all I have seen!"[15]

14. *Ātmā* is therefore called *idandra.*[16] His name is Idandra, but people indirectly call him Indra, for the gods love the cryptic.[17]

Second *Adhyāya*

Birth

1. An embryo begins as semen within a man. A man's vigor is collected in the form of semen from all parts of his body, and in this way he carries a new body within himself. When that man injects his semen into a woman, that new body is created. This is a person's first birth.

2-3. This new body then becomes part of the woman's body in a way that she is not harmed. And because she nourishes his embryo that has entered her, she herself should be nourished. In this way, she carries the man in the form of an embryo.[18] From the onset, therefore, a man nourishes a child even before its birth and thereby he nourishes himself. This is how the worlds continue. This is his second birth.

4. His new body[19] has been established in order to perform good deeds.[20] In this way his old body, having completed its course, dies, and so he leaves this world and is born again. This is his third birth.[21]

5. In this regard the sage has said:

Even laying as an embryo within the womb,
I came to know the births of these gods.
A hundred bonds, as if made of iron, caged me,[22]
And yet easily, like a hawk, I burst forth.

Vamadeva declared this even as he lay within his mother's womb.

6. And because he knew this, after fulfilling his desires in heavenly realms, obtained immortality upon the dissolution of his body.

Third *Adhyāya*

The *Ātmā*

1. So who is this one we respect as the *ātmā?* Which of these is the *ātmā*? Is it the one by which things are seen? Is it the one by which things are heard? Is it the one by which things are smelled? Is it the one by which words are spoken? Or is it the

---

[22] The words are *pura āyasī*. A *pura* is a castle or fort, and it is said to be surrounded by iron. Here the *pura* is a metaphor for the body. The spiritual soul is caged to its physical body, which holds it in an iron grip, so to speak.

[23] The word is *prājñāna,* which can be rendered as cognition, intelligence, knowledge, wisdom. It will be used extensively in the final lines of this Upanishad.

one by which things are tasted, sweet or unsweet?

2. Is it the heart? Is it the mind? Is it awareness, perception, or discernment? Is it cognition, wisdom, insight, steadfastness, thought, or reflection? Is it drive or memory, intention or purpose? Is it will, love, or desire? All these are but various forms of consciousness.[23]

3. It is *brahma*. It is Indra. It is Prajapati. It is all the gods. It is the five great elements: earth, wind, space, the waters and the lights. It is all these beings as well as those that are a mixture of smaller beings of various sorts – those born of eggs from wombs, from sweat, and from sprouts. It is horses, cattle, men, and elephants. It is everything that has life: those that move, those that fly, and those that are stationary.

All this world is guided by consciousness. In fact, this world is founded on consciousness. Consciousness is the eye and the foundation of this world. *Brahma* is consciousness.

4. And so with this understanding Vamadeva ascended from this world with his *ātmā* and, having fulfilled his desires in the heavenly worlds, attained immortality. Indeed, he became immortal!

Here ends the Aitareya Upanishad

3

Kaushitaki Upanishad

Introduction to

Kaushitaki Upanishad

The Kaushitaki Upanishad is part of the Kaushitaki Aranyaka, which is part of the Rig Veda. The Kaushitaki Aranyaka comprises fifteen chapters. Four of these chapters form the Kaushitaki Upanishad. The chronology of Kaushitaki Upanishad, like other Upanishads, is unclear, but this Upanishad appears to be pre-Buddhist and pre-Jain, yet later than the more ancient Brihad Aranyaka and Chandogya Upanishads. It is therefore likely that the Kaushitaki Upanishad is one of the middle Upanishads along with the Aitareya and Taittiriya Upanishads. This places the Kaushitaki Upanishad before the sixth century BCE. The Kaushitaki Upanishad is a prose text, divided into four chapters, containing six, fifteen, nine and twenty verses respectively.

---

[1] The word is *saṃvṛtam,* which means a hidden or secret place.

[2] Two paths will be described in this Upanishad, the path to *mokṣa* and the path that leads to rebirth. Here Citra Ganyayani is asking which path Shvetaketu will place him on.

First *Adhyāya*

1. When Citra Ganyayani wanted to perform a sacrifice, he chose Aruni Gautama as his priest. Aruni sent his son, Shvetaketu, saying, Please do the sacrifice on my behalf.

After Shvetaketu had taken his seat, Citra Ganyayani questioned him: O son of Gautama, can you show me that hidden path[1] that leads away from this world, or will you place me on one of the other paths?[2]

Shvetaketu replied, I do not know these things. Let me ask my father.

Shvetaketu returned to his father and said, How shall I answer these questions? His father replied, "Even I do not know the answer to these questions. So let us go together."

With fuel in hand, Aruni went to Citra Ganyayani and said, I wish to become your student.

Citra Ganyayani replied, O Gautama, because you have not succumbed to pride, you are worthy to know *brahma*. Come, I will teach you.

2. Citra Ganyayani spoke:

Those who depart this world first go to the moon. Due to the life force of these beings, the moon swells and becomes full during its first half. Then, during its second half, these beings are ejected from the moon and are reborn. Indeed, the moon is the gateway to heaven! Those who can answer the questions of the moon proceed to heaven, whereas those who cannot become rain and fall to earth. In this way beings are born into various species, to become worms, insects, fish, birds, lions, boar,

---

[3] A lunar month is divided into two halves, a waxing half and a waning half. Each lunar half has fifteen lunar days, known as *tithis*. Therefore, this is a reference to the moon.

[4] The moon is said to constantly be born and die as it cycles through its phases. It is therefore a symbol for rebirth.

[5] See footnote below. Just as the thirteenth month is special and held to be sacred, so is that person who is destined for *mokṣa*. Such a person is compared to the thirteenth month.

[6] The lunar year, like the solar year, is made of twelve months. The solar year has 365 days while the lunar year has only 354 days. Just as a leap year adds an extra day to the solar calendar every four years to correct for temporal alignment, so the lunar year adds an extra month, a thirteenth month, every two and a half years.This extra month is called *adhika-māsa*, extra month, and it is generally viewed as a sacred time. In fact, it is called *puruṣottama māsa*, God's month, in some parts of India.

[7] A moment is a measure of time known as a *muhūrta*, which lasts 48 minutes. There are 30 such *muhūrtas* in a 24-hour period and they each have a name and define a time of the day. The *yeṣṭiha muhūrha* is said to be a moment of heavenly time.

snakes, tigers, men, or some other species according to their deeds and learning.

Upon entering the moon, the man of knowledge may be asked, Who are you? So he should answer:

O seasons, you procure semen from that shining one, the moon, who is made of fifteen parts,[3] and who is constantly reborn,[4] and who is the shelter of ancestors. You place that semen into a man, who then acts as the agent and pours it into a mother.

I am the one who is born, who appears as the extra month,
the thirteenth month[5] of a father made of twelve parts.[6]
I know this! I understand this!
O seasons, carry me to immortality!

By this truth, by this austerity, I am the seasons. I am the offspring of the seasons. Who am I? I am you!

The moon allows him passage.

3. Taking the path to the gods, he first reaches the world of fire, then the worlds of the winds and waters, then the worlds of Indra and the progenitors, and finally he reaches the realm of *brahma*. In this place there is Lake Ara, the moments known as Yeshtiha,[7] the river Vijara, the tree Ilya, the plaza Salajya, the palace Aparajita, the doorkeepers Indra and Prajapati, the hall known as Vibhu, the throne Vicakshana, and the couch Amitaujas.

4a. The man of learning first approaches Lake Ara and crosses it with his mind. Those without full knowledge drown in this lake. He then comes to the moments, Yeshtiha, and they flee from him. Next he reaches the river Vijara, which he also crosses with his mind. There he shakes off his good and evil deeds. His favored relatives accrue his good deeds, whereas his evil deeds go to his unfavored relatives. It is like a person driving a chariot and who sees the two wheels. Such a person sees day and night, good and evil deeds, and all the dualities of life. Being free of both his good and evil deeds, the man of knowledge quickly arrives at the realm of *brahma.*

4b.The beloved Manasi and her twin, Cakshushi, along with other divine nymphs, including Jagati, Amba, Ambali and Ambika, bring him flowers. As this man of knowledge is approaching, *Brahmā*[8] himself calls out to them, Run to this man of my glory! He has already reached the river Vijara. He will never grow old! Five hundred divine nymphs go to greet him, a hundred carry garlands, a hundred carry lotions, a hundred carry

[8] There are two words, *brahman* and *brahman*, and even though they look identical, they are different. One is masculine and the other is neuter. The masculine *brahman* declines as Brahmā while the neuter *brahman* declines as *brahma*. In compound it is impossible to tell which *brahman* is intended. It is only by context that one or the other can be determined. The neuter *brahman* (*brahma*) is the idea of God as impersonal, as the all-pervasive force and substratum of all things. The masculine *brahman* (Brahmā) is the personification of that impersonal form of God. For contextual reasons, here I have elected to translate using the masculine form, Brahmā.

fragrant powders, a hundred carry garments and a hundred carry plates of fruits. They dress him with the ornaments of Brahmā. Thus, the man of knowledge is adorned with the ornaments of Brahmā and attains *brahma*.

5. He soon reaches the tree known as Ilya, where he is permeated with the fragrances of Brahmā. Next he reaches the plaza known as Salajya, wherein he is permeated with the flavors of Brahmā. Then he reaches the palace known as Aparajita, wherein the luster of Brahmā enters him. After this he reaches the two doorkeepers, Indra and Prajapati, who flee from him. The glory of Brahmā enters him as he arrives at the hall known as Vibhu.

Finally he arrives at Vicakshana, the throne. Its two front legs are the Sama chants, Brihat and Rathantara. Its two rear legs are the chants Shyaita and Naudhasa. Its lengthwise supports are the chants Vairupa and Vairaja, and its two side supports are the chants Shakvara and Raivata. This throne is wisdom, for by wisdom a man is able to see.

Then he arrives at the couch, Amitaujas. It is life-breath. Its two front legs are the past and the present, its two back legs are prosperity and nourishment, its two lengthwise supports are the Sama chants Bṛhat and Rathantara, its two head supports are the Sama chants Bhadra and Yajnayajniya, the strings stretching lengthwise are the Rig verses and the Sama chants. Those stretching crosswise are the Yajus formulas, the coverlet is the Soma stalks; the second cover is the High Chant, and the pillow is prosperity.

On that couch sits *Brahmā*. A man who knows this mounts it, first with his foot. Brahmā then asks him: Who are you? This man should reply:

6. I am the seasons. I am the offspring of the seasons. I am born from the womb of space. I am the seed for the wife. I am the radiance of the year. I am the soul of every being. And like you, who is the soul of every being, I am who you are.

Brahmā then asks him, And who am I?

The man of learning should answer, You are *satya*.[9]

Brahmā then asks, And what is *satya*?

He replies, *Sat* is that which is other than this body with its senses and life force. *Tya*[10] is the body with its senses and life force. This is what is understood by the word *satya*. In this way

---

[9] The word *satya* is made of the core word *sat* and the abstract suffix *ya*. Ordinarily it means trueness or truth. Here, however, the Upanishad is taking it as two distinct words, *sat* and *tya*. Two realms of existence are indicated, a higher reality called the Real (*sat*) and this physical world we see all around us suggested by the word *tya*. Literally, *tya* means "this," in the sense of "this, which you see before you." Thus, the word *satya* includes both that higher reality, which is unseen to most people, and this physical world that people see all around.

[10] See fn above.

all this is *satya* and you are all this. This is what he spoke to him.

In this verse it is declared:

7. Yajur is the belly, Sama is the head, and the Rig is the imperishable body. This is *brahma*. A great seer, who is full of *brahma,* knows this.

Then Brahmā asked him, By what means do you comprehend my masculine names?

He answers, By breath.

By what means do you apprehend my neuter names?

By the mind.

By what means do you apprehend my feminine names?

By speech.

By what means do you apprehend my fragrances?

By the nose.

By what means do you apprehend my forms?

By the eye.

By what means do you apprehend my sounds?

By the ear.

By what means do you apprehend my tastes?

By the tongue.

By what means do you apprehend my actions?

By my two hands.

By what means do you apprehend happiness and suffering?

By the body.

By what means do you apprehend the joys of procreation?

By the organ of generation.

By what means do you apprehend movement?

By my two feet.

---

[11] The word is *devatā*, divinities.

[12] The intended meaning here is that when one realizes his connection with *brahma* he no longer needs to endeavor separately for things. Whatever is required comes naturally.

By what means do you apprehend thoughts, perceptions, and desires?

By the intellect.

Brahmā finally said to him, This man has indeed attained my world. Whatever victory and success belongs to *brahma* also belongs to the man who knows this!

Here ends the First *Adhyāya*

Second *Adhyāya*

1. The sage Kaushitaki used to say, Breath is *brahma!*

When breath is known as *brahma,* the mind becomes the messenger, the eye becomes the protector, the ear becomes the proclaimer, and speech becomes the serving maid. Indeed, the person who knows this soon comes to possess a messenger, a protector, a proclaimer, and a serving maid.

And to this very breath, all the senses[11] bring tribute without asking. And likewise, to the man who knows this, all beings bring tribute without his asking. So here is the secret: One who knows *brahma* has no need to ask for anything.[12]

It is like a man who goes begging in a village, but receives nothing. In frustration, he sits alone and thinks, I am not going to receive anything from this village. But for one who knows *brahma*, suddenly those very people who at first rejected him call him to accept alms. So this is the rule for one who knows *brahma:* There is no necessity to ask for anything. Food givers automatically give food.[13]

2. The sage Paingya also used to say, Breath is *brahma*! Now, with regards to this breath there is speech; behind this speech there is sight; and behind sight there is hearing, behind hearing is the mind, and behind mind lies breath.[14]

Without being asked, all the divinities bring tribute to this breath. Similarly, for one who understands these things, all beings bring tribute to this knower of *brahma*. The secret here is that when one knows *brahma,* one need not ask for anything.

---

[13] Literally, "To you we give."

[14] This is why breath control is used to control the mind during meditation.

[15] I have provided the transliterated Sanskrit mantras instead of a translation because the power lies more with the mantras than the meaning. However, an approximate translation reads as follows: The deity named speech can capture what I want. May speech capture it for me from so-and-so. I glorify that deity.
"The deity named smell… .
"The deity named sight… .
"The deity named hearing… .
"The deity named mind… .
"The deity named intelligence… .

If a person comes to a village and goes begging, but receives nothing and so in frustration thinks, I will never eat in this village. Then the very same villagers who previously refused him will come forward and offer him invitations to eat. So this is the rule for the one who knows *brahma*: Charitable people will naturally come forward, saying, Let us give to him!

3. Now, if someone desires an object of value, he should meditate on that object. Then, on a full or new moon day or any another auspicious day, he should select an area, sweep and purify it with water and sacred grass, and then arrange a sacrificial fire. Sitting with legs crossed, he should make oblations into the fire with a sacrificial spoon while chanting:[15]

vāṅ nāma devatāvarodhanī sā me 'muṣmād idam avarundhyāt, tasyai svāhā

ghrāṇo nāma devatāvarodhanī sā me 'muṣmād idam avarundhyāt, tasyai svāhā

cakṣur nāma devatāvarodhanī sā me 'muṣmād idam avarundhyāt, tasyai svāhā

śrotraṃ nāma devatāvarodhanī sā me 'muṣmād idam avarundhyāt, tasyai svāhā

mano nāma devatāvarodhanī sā me 'muṣmād idam avarundhyāt, tasyai svāhā prājñā nāma devatāvarodhanī sā me 'muṣmād idam avarundhyāt, tasyai svāhā

Then, after he smells the fragrance of the smoke and smears melted butter on his body from the sacrificial fire, he should move about with resolution and make his objective known, either directly or through a messenger. In this way he will take possession of his object.

4. Similarly, to secure heavenly love: If someone desires the love of a particular man or woman, or of a group of men or women, he should make the same offerings of melted butter in the same manner on one of the auspicious days given above. He should then chant the following mantras:

vācaṃ te mayi juhomyasau svāhā[16]

ghrāṇaṃ te mayi juhomyasau svāhā

cakṣus te mayi juhomyasau svāhā

śrotraṃ te mayi juhomyasau svāhā

manas te mayi juhomyasau svāhā

---

[16] Here again the mantras are more important. An approximate translation: O, so-and-so (the name of the person whose love is desired), your speech I sacrifice in me, hail to you. … O, so- and-so, your breath… your eye… your mind… your intellect… .

prajñāṃ te mayi juhomyasau svāhā

Then, after he smells the fragrance of the smoke and smears melted butter on his body from the sacrificial fire, he should move about with resolution and make contact with the person(s) of his desire, or simply stand upwind engaged in conversation with that person(s) in question. He will become their favorite! They will indeed love him!

5. Next, according to Pratardana, the Agni Hotra fire sacrifice is a matter of internal sacrifice. When a person speaks, he is not able to breathe, and so at that time he offers the breath into speech. Similarly, when a person breathes, he is not able to speak, and so at that time he offers speech into breath.

In this way one makes a continuous, immortal offering regardless of whether one is awake or asleep. All other offerings are limited because they are dependent on some form of ritual action. For this reason, in ancient times the wise did not perform ritual offerings.

6. Shushkabhringara has said, The *ukta* is *brahma*. All beings, therefore, should venerate it as the Rig itself. Then, for the sake of his prosperity, all beings should recite praises for him. One should venerate it as the Yajus. Then, for the sake of his prosperity, all beings will unite with him. One should venerate it as the Sama. Then, for the sake of his prosperity, all beings will bow to him.

One should venerate this *ukta* as prosperity, glory and radiance. Then, just as the *uktha* is the most prosperous, glorious and splendid recitation, so someone who knows this becomes the most prosperous, glorious and splendid of all beings.

Now, upon this essence of the sacrifice, the *ukta*, the Adhvaryu priest prepares it and infuses it with the Yajus formulas. Then the Hotri priest infuses it with the Rig formulas. Finally, the Udgatri priest infuses it with the Sama formulas. In this way, this *ukta* becomes the essence of the three Vedas. The one who understands this becomes infused with the essence of the Vedas.

7. Next, there are three modes of veneration of Sarvajit Kaushitaki. This is how Sarvajit Kaushitaki used to venerate the rising sun. Wearing the upper garment in the sacrificial position, he would fetch some water, pour it into the water pot three times, and say, You are the one who gathers! Gather my sin! He used to worship the midday sun in exactly the same way, saying: You are the one who gathers up! Gather up my sin! And he used to worship the setting sun in exactly the same way, saying, You are the one who gathers completely! Gather my sin completely! And the sun did gather completely whatever sin he had committed by day or night.

Likewise, when a man knows this and worships the sun in exactly the same way, the sun gathers up whatever sin he may have committed by day or night.

---

[17] RV 1.91.16, 9.31.4, 1.91.18.

8. Every month, on the night of the new moon, one should worship the moon as it approaches the west, using the very same procedure. Or else one may throw two green blades of grass toward it, saying:

My gentle heart rests within this moon above. This I know, so may I never weep for my children's misfortune!

His children, indeed, will not die before him.

The preceding is for a man who has a son. As for one who does not have a son, he should first recite silently these three Rig verses:[17]

Swell up, O Soma! May virility gather in you from all sides! Be there at the gathering of power!

May juices and powers, may virile energies, gather in you, who crush your enemies. As you swell to immortality, O Soma, you capture the highest glory in the sky.

That tiny drop the Adityas make to swell. That imperishable drop, the immortal ones drink. With that drop may King Varuna and Brihaspati, the guardian gods of the world, make us prosper!

He then says: Do not swell up by means of our life-breath, our children, or our livestock. Swell up instead by means of the life-breath, children, and livestock of the man who hates us and whom we hate. Then he turns a full circle toward his right, saying: I turn the way of Indra! I turn the way of the sun!

9. On the night of the full moon, furthermore, one should worship the moon as it becomes visible in the east using the very same procedure, saying:

You are King Soma, the radiant! You are Prajapati, with five mouths! The *brāhmaṇa* is one of your mouths. With that mouth you eat kings. Make me a food-eater with that mouth.

The king is one mouth of yours. With that mouth you eat the Vaishyas. Make me a food-eater with that mouth.

The falcon is one mouth of yours. With that mouth you eat the birds. Make me a food-eater with that mouth.

The fire is one mouth of yours. With that mouth you eat this world. Make me a food-eater with that mouth.

There is a fifth mouth. With that mouth you eat all beings. Make me a food-eater with that mouth.

Do not wane by means of our life-breath, our children, or our livestock. Wane instead by means of the life, children, and livestock of the man who hates us and whom we hate. Then he turns a full circle toward his right, saying: I turn the way of the deities! I turn the way of the sun!

10. Now, when a man is preparing to engage in sexual inter-

course with his wife, he should touch her heart, saying:

Your heart, O lady so good to lie on, rests within Prajapati. Therefore, O queen of immortality, may you not encounter your children's misfortune!

Her children, indeed, will not die before her.

11. Now, when a man returns from a journey, he should sniff his son's head, saying:

From my body you spring!
From my heart you are born!
You're my self, son, you have rescued me!
May you live a hundred years!

With that he confers a name on him.

Be a rock! Be an ax!
Be indestructible gold!
You are the radiance called son!
May you live a hundred years!

With that he pronounces his son's name and then embraces him, saying: As Prajapati embraced his children for their safety, so I embrace you! Then he recites this silently in his son's right ear:

O Indra! O Maghavan! O Rijisin!
Grant him ample wealth, bestowing all treasures.

O Indra, you with fine cheeks!
Grant him a hundred years to live, and countless heroic sons.

And in his left ear:

Grant him, O Indra, the finest treasures and quickness of mind,
good fortune and increase of wealth,
bodily safety and sweetness of speech,
fine weather every day of his life.

Then he sniffs his son's head three times, saying:

Be not cut off! Do not weaken!
O my son, live a life, a hundred years long!
With your name, I kiss your head!

Then he makes the sound *hum* over his son's head, saying: With the same *hum* sound the cows make as they low,[18] I make the *hum* sound upon your head.

12. Next, the "dying of the deities."[19] *Brahma* shines forth here when the fire is burning, but, when the fire stops burning, it dis-

---

[18] The lowing of cattle is a low humming sound made over their young.

[19] Fire, the sun, the moon, and lightning, etc. are seen as deities, shining ones. Similarly, the senses are also considered as deities or shining ones. This idea of shining comes from the Sanskrit root *div*, to shine. The English words divinity and divine also come from the same route *div,* to shine.

appears, and its radiance goes to the sun and its life-breath to the wind. *Brahma* shines forth here when the sun is shining, but, when the sun stops shining, it disappears, and its radiance goes to the moon and its life-breath to the wind. *Brahma* shines forth here when the moon is shining, but, when the moon stops shining, it disappears, and its radiance goes to the lightning and its life-breath to the wind. *Brahma* shines forth here when the lightning is flashing, but, when the lightning stops flashing, it disappears, and its radiance goes to the quarters and its life-breath to the wind. Now, when they have entered into the wind, when they have crept into the wind, all these deities do not lose their self-identity, but emerge from it once again.

That was with respect to the deities. Next, with respect to the body:

13. *Brahma* shines forth when one speaks; but when one stops speaking, it disappears, and its radiance goes to one's sight and its life-breath to one's breath. *Brahma* shines forth when one sees; but when one stops seeing, it disappears, and its radiance goes to one's hearing and its life-breath to one's breath. *Brahma* shines forth when one hears; but when one stops hearing it disappears, and its radiance goes to one's mind and its life-breath to one's breath. *Brahma* shines forth when one thinks; but when one stops thinking, it disappears, and its radiance goes to one's breath, and its life-breath to one's breath. Now, when they have entered the breath, when they have crept into the breath, all these deities do not lose their self-identity, but emerge from it once again.

And, therefore, when someone knows this, even if both mountain ranges, the southern and the northern, were to rush at him determined to crush him, they would not succeed in crushing him. On the contrary, the people who hate him and the people he himself hates will die around him.

14. Next, who is preeminent. Once upon a time these deities, each arguing for their own preeminence, departed from this body, and it lay there like a clod.

Then speech entered the body; but although it spoke with its speech, it still remained there lying prostrate.

After that sight entered the body, but, although it spoke with its speech and saw with its sight, it still remained there lying prostrate.

After that hearing entered the body; but although it spoke with its speech, saw with its sight, and heard with its hearing, it still remained there lying prostrate.

After that the mind entered the body; but although it spoke with its speech, saw with its sight, heard with its hearing, and thought with its mind, it still remained there lying prostrate.

Finally, breath entered the body, and straightaway it got up.

After all these deities had recognized the preeminence of breath and united themselves with that very breath, which is the essence of intelligence, they all departed from this body and, entering the wind and with space as their self, went to heaven.

In exactly the same way, a person who knows this, after he has recognized the preeminence of breath and united himself with that breath, which is the essence of intelligence, departs from this body accompanied by all these and, entering the wind and with space as his self, goes to heaven. He goes to where these gods are. And because the gods are immortal, upon reaching there a man who knows this becomes immortal.

15. Next, the father-son ceremony, which is also called the rite of transference. A father, when he is close to death, calls his son. After the house has been strewn with fresh grass, the fire has been kindled and a pot of water has been set down along with a cup, the father lies down covered in a fresh garment. The son comes and lies on top of him, touching the various organs of the father with his own corresponding organs. Alternatively, the father may execute the transfer with the son sitting and facing him. The father then makes the transfer to the son:

I place my speech in you, says the father. I place your speech in me, responds the son.

I place my breath in you, says the father. I place your breath in me, responds the son.

I place my sight in you, says the father. I place your sight in me, responds the son.

I place my hearing in you, says the father. I place your hearing in me, responds the son.

I place my tasting of food in you, says the father. I place your tasting of food in me, responds the son.

I place my actions in you, says the father. I place your actions in me, responds the son.

I place my pleasures and pains in you, says the father. I place your pleasures and pains in me, responds the son.

I place my bliss, delight, and procreation in you, says the father. I place your bliss, delight, and procreation in me, responds the son.

I place my movements in you, says the father. I place your movements in me, responds the son.

I place my mind in you, says the father. I place your mind in me, responds the son.

I place my intelligence in you, says the father. I place your intelligence in me, responds the son.

If he finds it difficult to talk, the father should briefly say: I place my vital functions in you. And the son should respond: I place your vital functions in me.

Then, as the son, turning around toward his right, goes away toward the east, his father calls out to him: May glory, the luster of sacred knowledge, and fame attend you! The son, for his part, looks over his left shoulder, hiding his face with his hand or covering it with the hem of his garment, and responds: May you gain heavenly worlds and realize your desires!

If the father recovers his health, he should either live under the authority of his son or live as a wandering ascetic. But if he happens to die, they should perform the appropriate final rites for him.

Here ends the Second *Adhyāya*

Third *Adhyāya*

1. Once Pratardana, the son of Divodasa, arrived at the esteemed residence of Indra. Indra said to him, Choose a boon, Pratardana.

But Pratardana replied, Why don't you yourself choose something for me that you consider most beneficial to a human being?

Indra replied, Surely, a superior does not choose for an inferior. You had better choose for yourself.

Pratardana replied, I think I'll do without the boon. Indra, however, did not deviate from the truth, for Indra is the truth.

So Indra told Pratardana, What I consider to be most beneficial to a human being is that he should understand me. After all I killed the three-headed son of Tvastri,[20] as well as the Arunmukhas. I handed over the Yatis to the hyenas. I smashed the Prahladiyas in the sky, the Paulomas in the intermediate region, and the Kalakanjas on the earth. And I did not lose even a hair of my body in the process.

When a man understands me, nothing that he does—whether it is stealing, or performing an abortion, or killing his own father or mother—will ever make him lose a single hair of his body. And when he has committed a sin, his face does not lose its color.

2. Indra continued: I am breath, the soul, consisting of intelligence. So venerate me as life and immortality. Breath is life. And life is breath, for as long as breath remains in this body, so does life; and hence it is through breath that one attains immortality, and, through intelligence, true intentions. Anyone who venerates me as life and immortality gets to live his full life span in this world and wins an immortal and imperishable state in the heavenly world.

Indra continued: But there are some who say that the vital functions come together into a unified whole. For no one is able to bring himself to perceive separately a name with his speech, a visible appearance with his sight, a sound with his hearing, or a

[20] This story is first found in RV 10.8.89.

thought with his mind. When the vital functions have become a unified whole, however, they make him perceive all these one by one—as speech speaks, all the vital functions speak along with it; as sight sees, all the vital functions see along with it; as hearing hears, all the vital functions hear along with it; as the mind thinks, all the vital functions think along with it; and as the breath breathes, all the vital functions breathe along with it.

This may be so, continued Indra. But among the vital functions there is one that is preeminent.

3. A man continues to live after his speech leaves him, for we see people who are dumb. A man continues to live after his sight leaves him, for we see people who are blind. A man continues to live after his hearing leaves him, for we see people who are deaf. A man continues to live after his mind leaves him, for we see people who are imbeciles. And a man continues to live after his arms are cut off and after his legs are cut off, for we see such people.

But only the breath, you see, is the self consisting of intelligence. When it grasps this body, it enables the body to get up (*uttha*), and for this reason one should venerate it as the *ukta*. This is how one comes to possess the Whole in one's breath.

Now, breath is intelligence, and intelligence is breath. One comes to perceive this in the following way. When a man is fast asleep and sees no dreams at all, then these become unified within this very breath. His speech then merges into it together with all the names; his sight merges into it together with all the visible appearances; his hearing merges into it together with all the sounds; and his mind merges into it together with all the thoughts. And when he awakens these fly off. As from a blazing fire sparks fly off in every direction, so from this self the vital functions fly off to their respective stations; and from the vital functions, the gods; and from the gods, the worlds.

When this very breath that is the self consisting of intelligence grasps this body, it enables the body to get up (*uttha*), and for this reason one should venerate it as the *ukta*. This is how one comes to possess the Whole in one's breath.

Breath is intelligence, and intelligence is breath. One comes to perceive this in the following way. When a man is sick and about to die, he becomes extremely weak and finally loses consciousness. People then say:

Has his breath, perhaps, already left him? At this point, he ceases to hear, he ceases to see, he ceases to speak with his speech, and he ceases to think. Then these become unified within this very breath. His speech merges into it together with all the names; his sight merges into it together with all the visible appearances; his hearing merges into it together with all the sounds; and his mind merges into it together with all the thoughts. And when the breath finally departs from this body, it is together with all these that it departs.

4. Speech releases from this breath all the names, and through

speech one grasps all the names. The sense of smell releases from it all the odors, and through the sense of smell one grasps all the odors. Sight releases from it all the visible appearances, and through sight one grasps all the visible appearances. Hearing releases from it all the sounds, and through hearing one grasps all the sounds. The mind releases from it all the thoughts, and through the mind one grasps all the thoughts. This is how one comes to possess the Whole in one's breath. Breath is intelligence, and intelligence is breath, for they both live in this body together, and together they depart from it.

Next, we will explain how, [drawn] from this intelligence, all beings become one.

5. Speech is one part drawn from it, and name is the particle of being that corresponds externally to speech. The sense of smell is one part drawn from it, and odor is the particle of being that corresponds externally to the sense of smell. Sight is one part drawn from it, and visible appearance is the particle of being that corresponds externally to sight. Hearing is one part drawn from it, and sound is the particle of being that corresponds externally to hearing. The tongue is one part drawn from it, and the taste of food is the particle of being that corresponds externally to the tongue. The hands are one part drawn from it, and action is the particle of being that corresponds externally to the hands. The body is one part drawn from it, and pleasure and pain constitute the particle of being that corresponds externally to the body. The sexual organ is one part drawn from it, and bliss, delight, and procreation constitute the particle of being

that corresponds externally to the sexual organ. The feet are one part drawn from it, and movements constitute the particle of being that corresponds externally to the feet. Intelligence is one part drawn from it, and thoughts, objects of perception, and desires constitute the particle of being that corresponds externally to the intelligence.

6. When someone takes control of speech by means of intelligence,[21] he grasps all names through his speech. When someone takes control of the sense of smell by means of intelligence, he grasps all odors through his sense of smell. When someone takes control of sight by means of intelligence, he grasps all visible appearances through his sight. When someone takes control of hearing by means of intelligence, he grasps all sounds through his hearing. When someone takes control of the tongue by means of intelligence, he grasps all tastes of food through his tongue. When someone takes control of the hands by means of intelligence, he grasps all actions through his hands. When someone takes control of the body by means of intelligence, he grasps pleasures and pains through his body. When someone takes control of the sexual organ by means of intelligence, he grasps bliss, delight, and procreation through his sexual organ. When someone takes control of the feet by means of intelligence, he grasps all movements through his feet. When someone takes control of thinking by means of intelligence, he grasps thoughts, objects of perception, and desires through his intelligence.

---

[21] The word used here is *prajñā*, which means intellect, discernment or even wisdom.

7. For without intelligence, speech would not make someone perceive any name. So, one says: My mind was elsewhere. I did not perceive that name. For without intelligence, the sense of smell would not make someone perceive any odor. So one says: My mind was elsewhere. I did not perceive that odor. For without intelligence, sight would not make someone perceive any visible appearance. So one says: My mind was elsewhere. I did not perceive that visible appearance. For without intelligence, hearing would not make someone perceive any sound. So one says: My mind was elsewhere. I did not perceive that sound. For without intelligence, the tongue would not make someone perceive the taste of any food. So one says: My mind was elsewhere. I did not perceive the taste of that food. For without intelligence, the hands would not make someone perceive any action. So one says: My mind was elsewhere. I did not perceive that action. For without intelligence, the body would not make someone perceive any pleasure or pain. So one says: My mind was elsewhere. I did not perceive that pleasure or that pain. For without intelligence, the sexual organ would not make someone perceive any bliss, delight, or procreation. So one says: 'My mind was elsewhere. I did not perceive that bliss, delight, or procreation. For without intelligence, the feet would not make someone perceive any movement. So, one says: My mind was elsewhere. I did not perceive that movement. For without intelligence, no thinking could take place, and one would not perceive any object of perception.

8. It is not the speech that a man should seek to apprehend; rather, he should get to know the one who speaks it. It is not the

odor that a man should seek to apprehend; rather, he should get to know the one who smells it. It is not the visible appearance that a man should seek to apprehend; rather, he should get to know the one who sees it. It is not the sound that a man should seek to apprehend; rather, he should get to know the one who hears it. It is not the taste of food that a man should seek to apprehend; rather, he should get to know the one who apprehends the taste of food. It is not the action that a man should seek to apprehend; rather, he should get to know the one who performs it. It is not the pleasure and pain that a man should seek to apprehend; rather, he should get to know the one who apprehends pleasure and pain. It is not the bliss, delight, or procreation that a man should seek to apprehend; rather, he should get to know the one who apprehends bliss, delight, or procreation. It is not the movement that a man should seek to apprehend; rather, he should get to know the one who moves. It is not the mind that a man should seek to apprehend; rather, he should know the one who thinks.

Here ends the Third *Adhyāya*

Fourth *Adhyāya*[22]

1. Gargya Balaki was a learned man who had traveled too many places including the lands of Ushinara, Satvan, Matsya, Kuru Pancala, Kashi and Videha. Once he visited Ajatashatru, the king of Kashi[23], and said to him: Let me explain *brahma* to you.

[22] The source of this chapter is likely BU 2.1.

[23] Modern-day Benares.

Ajatashatru replied: I'll give you a thousand cows! With a speech such as this, people are sure to rush here, shouting: Another Janaka! Another Janaka!

2. Balaki began:

In the sun it is greatness;
In the moon it is food;
In lightning it is radiance;
In thunder it is booming sound;
In the wind it is Indra;
In space it is vastness;
In fire it is destruction;
and in waters it is truth.

All this is in respect to the divinities.

Now in respect to the body:

In a mirror it is the reflection;
In a shadow it is the double;
In an echo it is life;
In sound it is death;
In a dream it is Yama, the god of death;
In the body it is Prajapati;
In the right eye it is speech;
In the left eye it is truth.

3. Balaki then said: It is that person in the sun whom I see.

Ajatashatru replied: Don't drag me into a discussion about him! I see him only as the most eminent of all beings, as their head. Anyone who sees him in this way will become the most eminent of all beings. He will become their head.

4. Balaki then said: It is that person in the moon that I see.

Ajatashatru replied: Don't drag me into a discussion about him! I see him only as Soma, the great king dressed in white, the essence of food. Anyone who sees him in this way will become the essence of food.

5. Balaki then said: It is that person in lightning that I see.

Ajatashatru replied: Don't drag me into a discussion about him! I see him only as the essence of radiance. Anyone who sees him in this way will become the essence of radiance.

6. Balaki then said: It is that person in thunder that I see.

Ajatashatru replied: Don't drag me into a discussion about him! I venerate him only as the essence of sound. Anyone who venerates him in this way will become the essence of sound.

7. Balaki then said: It is that person in the wind that I see.

Ajatashatru replied: Don't drag me into a discussion about him! I see him only as Indra, with the invincible weapon. Anyone who sees him in this way will become victorious and invincible, and he will triumph over his adversaries.

8. Balaki then said: It is that person in space that I see.

Ajatashatru replied: Don't drag me into a discussion about him! I see him only as the full and non-depleting *brahma*. Anyone who sees him in this way will become filled with children and livestock, with fame and the luster of sacred knowledge, and with the heavenly world. He will live his full life span.

9. Balaki then said: It is that person in the fire that I see.

Ajatashatru replied: Don't drag me into a discussion about him! I see him only as the irresistible one. Anyone who sees him in this way will become irresistible among those who are outsiders.

10. Balaki then said: It is that person in the waters that I see.

Ajatashatru replied: Don't drag me into a discussion about him! I see him only as the essence of truth. Anyone who sees him in this way will become the essence of truth.

That was with respect to the divinities. Next, with respect to the body.

11. Balaki then said: It is that person in the mirror that I see.

Ajatashatru replied: Don't drag me into a discussion about him! I see him only as a reflection. When anyone sees him in this way, only children who resemble him will be born to him, and none who does not resemble him.

12. Balaki then said: It is that person in a shadow that I see.

Ajatashatru replied: Don't drag me into a discussion about him! I see him only as the inseparable companion. Anyone who sees him in this way will find a companion; he will be a man who has a companion.

13. Balaki then said: It is that person in an echo that I see.

Ajatashatru replied: Don't drag me into a discussion about him! I see him only as life. Anyone who sees him in this way will not lose consciousness before his appointed time.

14. Balaki then said: It is that person in a sound that I see.

Ajatashatru replied: Don't drag me into a discussion about him! I see him only as death. Anyone who sees him in this way will not die before his appointed time.

15. Balaki then said: It is that person who, as one sleeps, roams about in dreams that I see.

Ajatashatru replied: Don't drag me into a discussion about him! I venerate him only as King Yama. When anyone sees him in this way, this whole world submits itself to his supremacy.

16. Balaki then said: It is that person in the body that I see.

Ajatashatru replied: Don't drag me into a discussion about him! I see him only as Prajapati. Anyone who sees him in this way propagates himself through children and livestock, fame and the luster of sacred knowledge, and the heavenly world; he will live his full life span.

17. Balaki then said: It is that person in the right eye that I see.

Ajatashatru replied: Don't drag me into a discussion about him! I see him only as the essence of speech, as the essence of fire, as the essence of light. Anyone who sees him in this way will become the essence of all these.

18. Balaki then said: It is that person in the left eye that I see.

Ajatashatru, replied: Don't drag me into a discussion about him! I see him only as the essence of truth, as the essence of lightning, as the essence of radiance. Anyone who sees him in this way will become the essence of all these.

19. Thereupon, Balaki fell silent. Is that all, Balaki? asked Ajatashatru.

That is all, replied Balaki

Ajatashatru then said to him: In vain have you dragged me into this discussion by saying, Let me declare *brahma* to you. It is the one who is the maker of the persons you have talked about in succession, whose handiwork they are, that you alone should seek to know, O Balaki.

Balaki then approached him, carrying firewood in his hands, and said: I come to you as your student.

But Ajatashatru said to him: I consider it a total reversal for a *brāhmaṇa* to become a student of a *kṣatriya*, However, I'll see to it that you perceive it clearly. Taking Balaki by the hand, they approached a sleeping man. Ajatashatru greeted the man in these words: O Soma, great king dressed in white! But he continued sleeping. Then Ajatashatru prodded him with a stick. Immediately the man got up.

Ajatashatru then asked: Balaki, where was this person who was lying down? Where is he now? And from where did he come? Balaki did not know. So Ajatashatru told him: To answer your questions where this person was lying down, and where he is now, and where he came from, in a person there are veins called *hitas* that extend from the heart to the pericardium. They are as fine as a hair split a thousandfold. They contain fluids of different colors, orange, white, black, yellow and red. When a person is asleep and sees no dreams, he remains within these veins.

20. At this time one's being has become concentrated within his life-breath, speech has merged into breath along with all the names; sight has merged into it along with visible appearance, hearing has merged into it along with sound, and mind has

merged into it along with thought. And when he awakens they scatter, like sparks flying out from a blazing fire. In the same way, from this life-breath the vital functions fly out to their respective places, and from there to the senses, and from the senses to the world.

This breath, which is the *ātmā* consisting of intelligence, pervades this body up to its very hairs and nails. Like a razor within its case or a termite within a termite hill, so this *ātmā* pervades this body up to its very hairs and nails. To this *ātmā* cling the senses just as servants to a chief. It is like this, just as a chief makes use of his own people and his own people make themselves useful to their chief, so this *ātmā* consisting of intelligence makes use of these senses and these senses make themselves useful to this *ātmā*.

For as long as Indra did not understand this *ātmā*, the demons prevailed over him. But when he came to understand, he smashed the demons, conquered them, and secured supremacy over all the gods. Similarly, a person who knows this removes all evils and secures supremacy over all beings. Indeed, he secures supremacy over all beings!

Here ends the Fourth *Adhyāya*

Here ends the Kaushitaki Upanishad

4

Kena Upanishad

Introduction to

Kena Upanishad

On Knowing *Brahma*

The Kena Upanishad is also known as the Talavakara Upanishad. It belongs to the Sama Veda. Talavakara is the name of the *brāhmana* of the Sama Veda to which this Upanishad belongs. The name of the Upanishad comes from the first word of this Upanishad, *kena*. It has four chapters known as *khandas*. The first two chapters are in verse and describe *brahma* as essentially unknowable and inexpressible. The final two chapters are in prose and show how the gods and their powers have come from *brahma*.

First *Khaṇḍa*

1. Who sets the mind in motion? Who keeps it going?[1]
Who initiates the first breath?
Who drives the world to speech?
What god engages the eye and the ear?

2. It is the hearer within the ear, the thinker within the mind, the speaker within speech, the breather within breath, and the seer within sight.

Knowing this, the wise free themselves from this world and become immortal.

3. Sight cannot see it; speech cannot describe it; mind cannot think it. We do not know or even understand how this can be taught.

4. Indeed, it is something that cannot be known. It is above what is knowable. This we have heard from the ancients who have explained it.

5. That which cannot be expressed with speech, but which is the foundation of speech,

---

[1] The first three lines of this verse begin with the word "*kena*", which may be translated as "by what," or "by whom." The first sentence, therefore, could be translated, "What drives the mind?" and so forth.

know that as *brahma,* and not what people ordinarily regard as speech.

6. That which cannot be thought, but which is the foundation of thought, know that as *brahma,* and not what people ordinarily regard as thought.

7. That which cannot be seen with the eye, but which is the foundation of seeing, know that as *brahma,* and not what people ordinarily regard as sight.

8. That which cannot be heard with the ear, but which is the foundation of hearing, know that as *brahma* and not what people ordinarily regard as sound.

---

[2] Which is to say, "the outer world."

[3] Here the word is *pratibhodha*, an awakening or insight.

[4] Here the word is *ātmā*, which I have translated as body or mind, but it could also be rendered as a reflexive pronoun, one's own self.

[5] Here the word is *vidyā,* knowledge or philosophy.

[6] Here the word is *satya*, which could also be rendered as *sat-ya*, realness. The more common translation is "truth."

9. That which breathes not with breath, but which is the foundation of breath, know that as *brahma,* and not what people ordinarily regard as breath.

Second *Khaṇḍa*

1. Teacher: If you say, "I know *brahma,*" only slightly do you know *brahma*. Indeed, you know only the outer appearance of *brahma* as it is defined by man and the gods.[2] So you must reflect upon what you do not know.

2. Student: I do not think, "I know It well," nor do I think, "I do not know It." The person amongst us who knows It, only thinks he knows It. In fact, he does not know what he does not know."

3. Teacher: It is only understood by one who does not understand It. The person who thinks he understands It knows It not. It is not understood by those who think they understand It. It is only understood by those who do not understand It.

4. It is known by an awakening;[3] only in that way can it be understood. Truly, one then finds immortality. Through the body and mind[4] one finds power, but through knowledge[5] one finds immortality.

5. While living in this world, if one knows It, then there is truth.[6] If one does not know it while living here, then it is a great loss. Seeing It in every being, the wise, on departing this world, become immortal and joyful.

Third *Khaṇḍa*[7]

1 Indeed, *brahma*[8] won a victory for the gods. The gods celebrated the victory of *brahma* and amongst themselves thought, "Truly, this is our victory; we are great!"

2. *Brahma* knew this and appeared before them, but they could not understand what it was. They said, "What wonderful thing[9] is this?"

3. They said to Fire, "O Jatavedas,[10] find out what this wonderful thing is."

"So be it."

4. Fire ran to *brahma.* It spoke to him: "Who are you? I am Fire, I am Jatavedas," he said.

5. *Brahma* inquired, "What power do you have?"

---

[7] Stylistically the Kena Upanishad is divided into two parts, the verse part (chapters 1 and 2) and the prose part (chapters 3 and 4). This is the beginning of the prose part.

[8] The word *brahma* is neuter, and although the word is used as a person, this is not to be construed as the creator god Brahmā. The reference here is to the impersonal "force" *brahma.*

[9] *Yakṣa*, a spirit, a ghost, an apparition.

[10] Jatavedas: a commonly used name for fire.

He replied, "I can burn everything on this earth."

6. *Brahma* placed some straw before him, "Burn this!"

He went at it with all speed, but he could not burn it. Thereupon Fire returned, saying, "I have not been able to find out what this wonderful thing is."

7. So they said to the wind, "O Vayu, find out what this wonderful thing is."

"So be it."

8. The wind ran towards *brahma* and It spoke to him, "Who are you?"

"I am the wind, Vayu; I am Matarishvan."

9. "What power do you have?"

The wind replied, "I can carry off everything in this world."

10. *Brahma* put some straw before him and said, "Carry this off!"

He went at it with all speed, but he was not able to carry it off. Thereupon the wind returned saying, "I have not been able to find out what this wonderful thing is."

11. So they said to Indra, "O Maghavan, find out what this wonderful thing is."

"So be it."

He ran towards It, but *brahma* disappeared from him.

12. Then, in the sky,[11] Indra came upon a woman of exceeding beauty called Uma, the daughter of the mountain.[12] Indra said to her, "What was that wonderful thing?"

---

[11] *ākāṣa*: sky, space

[12] The word *haimvati* means "daughter of Himavat", a mountain.

[13] See BU 5.6.1 for an earlier reference to lightning as *brahma.*

[14] The word for divinity here is *adhidaiva: adhi* is a prefix to verbs and nouns used to express "over" and "above"; *daiva* means '"relating to *deva,"* a god. Thus, *adhidaiva* is an experience of divinity.

[15] *Adhyātmā*: in Bhagavad Gita 8.3 this word is defined as *svabhāva*, one individual nature.

[16] *Upasmarati*: literally "remembers."

[17] *Sankalpa*: a mental intention or idea in the mind.

[18] The expression here is *tad-vana,* which is obscure. *Tad* is "that," and *vana* is "a forest" or "wood." This makes no obvious sense, so many commentators derive the word *vana* from *vāñch*, meaning to desire. This makes contextual sense, so I have translated *tad-vana* as "longing for this." The intended sense is that a desire to know *brahma* is the greatest thing in life.

[19] "Should be sought" is from *upasāritavya,* to be honored or attended upon.

[20] The word for sacred teaching is *upaniṣad*, mystic teaching.

Fourth *Khaṇḍa*

1. "It was *brahma,*" she said. "Rejoice in the victory of *brahma.*" Thereupon, he understood: "It was *brahma.*"

2. Therefore, Agni, Vayu, and Indra surpass, as it were, the other gods, for they got close to *brahma*, and they were the first to realize: "It is *brahma.*"

3. Indeed, Indra surpasses even the other gods because he got closest to It and he was the first to realize: "It is *brahma.*"

4. Here is a teaching in this regard: "The flash of the lightning[13] in the sky that causes one to blink and say, 'Ah!'– that Ah is divinity!"[14]

5. Similarly, regarding oneself:[15] That flash which comes to the mind as insight,[16] that burst of understanding,[17] that too is divinity!

6. The longing for this[18] should be sought.[19] All beings yearn for one who knows *brahma.*

7. O Sir, please tell me the sacred teaching.[20]

This sacred teaching has now been explained. Indeed, we have told you the sacred teaching of *brahma.*

8. Austerity, self-restraint, and work are the foundation of this mystic doctrine. The Vedas are its limbs. Truth is its abode.

9. One who truly knows this mystic doctrine, upon striking off all evil, becomes established in that most excellent, endless, heavenly world. Indeed he thrives and he prospers!

Here ends the Kena Upanishad

5

Katha Upanishad

Introduction to

Katha Upanishad

The Katha Upanishad is part of the Yajurveda. It is a theological text consisting of six chapters called Vallīs. Here's a brief summary:

The Upanishad begins with a story about a young boy named Nachiketa, who is sent to the abode of Yama (the god of death) by his father. Nachiketa waits three days for Yama's return. Impressed by his dedication, Yama offers him three boons. Nachiketa's first boon is peace with his father. The second is the knowledge of a fire sacrifice that leads to heaven. The third boon is the inquiry into the nature of life after death. Yama tries to dissuade Nachiketa from his third boon, offering worldly pleasures instead, but Nachiketa insists. This leads to a theological discourse. Yama teaches Nachiketa about the nature of the *ātmā* and its relationship with *brahma*. The Upanishad concludes with an affirmation of the power and importance of spiritual knowledge in attaining eternal peace and liberation.

First *Vallī*

Dialogue with Death

1-2. Once Ushan, the son of Vajashrava, performed the Vishvajit sacrifice and so prepared himself to give away all his possessions.[1] Understanding what his father was preparing to do, his son, Naciketas, became fearful[2] seeing the gifts his father was about to give.

[Naciketas thought]
3. These cows are barren. They are milked-out and old! A person who gives away such useless cows can only attain joyless worlds.

4. He said to his father: "Considering that I too am your possession, to whom shall you give me?" Three times he asked this question, "To whom shall you give me?" Finally, his father replied, "I give you to death!"

5-6. While on his way to the house of Death, Naciketas reflected: I go as the first of many. I go as the middling of many.

---

[1] Presumably Ushan was preparing to take *sannyāsa* and so renounce the world along with all his worldly possessions.

[2] The expression is *śraddhā-viveśa*, which is literally "faith entered." The son became fearful because he realized the offerings his father was preparing to give away were of poor quality, in this case milked-out cows. Giving this kind of gift would lead to hell instead of heaven. Therefore, he was afraid for his father's future.

What will Yama, the god of death, do with me? Look ahead. Look behind. Like grains, mortal man ripens and then falls to the ground only to be born again.

[Narrator]
7-8. A brahmin enters the home as a guest and, like fire, he must be appeased, "Bring water!"[3] Only the foolish allows a brahmin to remain within the home without food or drink. For such a person, all their hopes, expectations, fellowship, goodwill, rites, gifts, and even progeny and livestock soon fade away.

9. [Death]
For three nights you have remained in my home as a guest without food or water. O brahmin, forgive me, bless me. Choose three wishes!

[Naciketas]
10. May my father be pacified and become free of anger towards me when you have released me. This is my first wish.

---

[3] As fire is extinguished by water, so a guest in the home is appeased with hospitality.

[4] *Nihitam guhāyām. Guhā* is literally a cave. Commentators often take this as the heart—that this knowledge is hidden within the hearts of all.

[5] The meaning is obscure. The word is *śṛṅkā,* and it is only found in this Upanishad, and then only in two places (see 2.3). It has two meanings, a pathway and a string of jewels.

[Death]
11. Your father will indeed recognize you once I have released you. He will sleep peacefully at night and be free of anger once he has seen that you have been freed from the bonds of death.

[Naciketas]
12. In heaven there is no fear of old age because you are not there. There is no hunger, thirst or suffering. One enjoys in heaven!

13. You know the fire sacrifice that leads to heaven. I have faith, so please teach me how the residents of heaven enjoy immortality. This is my second wish.

[Death]
14. Naciketas, I shall explain to you what I know concerning the fire that leads to heaven. Listen carefully as I speak. Know this fire to be the means to attain an infinite world. This knowledge is at the foundation of the world and is hidden in the most secret place.[4]

[Narrator]
15. Death explained to Naciketas the details of this primal fire: the type of bricks it should have, how many, and how they should be laid. Naciketas repeated what he learned. The great soul, Death, was pleased with Naciketas and so spoke:

[Death]
16. I give you one further wish. From here on, this fire shall be named after you. It will be known as the *nāciketas* fire. Take this blazing fire as your pathway[5] to immortality.

17. One who has completed three *nāciketas* fires, who has been instructed by the three[6] and who has performed the three,[7] rises above birth and death. This fire[8] is the shining god born of *brahma*. When one understands this and is able to build this fire, one can attain supreme peace.

18. Again, one who has performed three *nāciketas* fires, and who has understood the three and who knows how to construct this fire altar, is able to drive away the bonds of death that confront him. Such a person becomes free of sorrow and delights in the heavenly worlds.

19. So, Naciketas, this is your fire which leads to heaven and this is what you have chosen for your second wish. People will proclaim this as your fire. Now please choose your third wish.

[Naciketas]
20. When a man dies there are doubts as to his condition. Some say he continues to exist; others say he ceases to exist. Please instruct me on this matter. This is my third wish.

---

[6] The meaning is obscure. One suggestion is that the three are the mother, the father, and the teacher. Another is *śruti*, *smriti*, and *sadhu*. Another is the three Vedas.

[7] Again the meaning is obscure. One suggestion is sacrifice, study, and almsgiving.

[8] The words are *brahma-ja-jñaṃ devam*. This is literally "the god who knows what is born of *brahma*."

[Death]
21. This matter is subtle and not easily understood. Even the gods have doubts about this. Choose another wish, Naciketas. Do not push me on this. Release me from this question.

[Naciketas]
22. What you say is true. This matter is not easily understood. Even the gods are confounded by this question. But there is no better teacher than you, O Death, and there is no better question than this.

[Death]
23. Choose sons and grandsons who live a hundred years. Choose livestock, elephants, horses and gold. Acquire a vast empire! Choose as many autumns as you wish.

24. And if you can imagine something even better, choose that along with wealth and a long life. Become king of all the earth, O Naciketas! I will make it so. I can fulfill all your desires.

25. Whatever you desire, even the most difficult things, just ask and I will fulfill your desires. Choose these lovely ladies who parade before us with music and song. Men cannot easily obtain such beings. I give them to you. Enjoy it all! Just don't ask me about the mysteries of death, Naciketas.

[Naciketas]
26. This mortal world, O Death, is fleeting. Even a full life is a short life. Such things you offer simply rob the vitality of the

senses. Keep your vehicles. Keep your song and dance.

27. A man can never be satisfied by wealth alone. How can we enjoy our wealth when we see you? We can only keep our life as long as you allow. So this is my final wish.

28. I have met beings who are immortal and who are never subject to old age and death. So what mortal being on this earth, who is subject to old age and death, could actually delight in a long life of fleeting pleasures and enjoyment?

28. O Death, please tell me about the great crossing. Beings in this world have doubts on this matter. I wish to penetrate this mystery. Naciketas wishes for nothing more than this!

Here ends the First *Vallī*

---

[9] See the ftn on 1.16. The word *sṛṅkā,* as noted before is obscure and only found in this Upanishad.

[10] Literally *vidyā* and *avidyā* are knowledge and ignorance. In this context they can be understood as spiritual knowledge and material knowledge. Compare this use of the terms *vidyā* and *avidyā* with the Isha Upanishad verses 9-11.

[11] *Avidyā* is to be construed with *preyas* and *vidyā* with śreyas. Here *avidya* is said to have the nature of desire and striving, while *vidyā* consists of detachment, truth and knowledge.

Second *Vallī*

[Death]

1. There are two paths, *śreyas:* the path of long-term good; and *preyas*, the path of immediate gain. They each have different results. Both bind a person. Between the two, *śreyas* gives what is best. One who chooses *preyas* fails to fulfill life's goals.

2. *Śreyas* and *preyas* both present themselves to a person. The wise one studies both and then chooses *śreyas*. Only a dullard chooses *preyas* for the sake of worldly pleasure.

3. But you, Naciketas, have considered all these pleasures and desires, and you have rejected this path, which is like a chain of jewels[9] that pulls men down.

4. What is known as *vidyā* and *avidyā*[10] are distinct and far removed from each other.[11] They are opposites! I see that Naciketas desires *vidyā*. All the pleasures and desires I have offered have not tempted him.

5. Wallowing in *avidyā* but calling themselves wise, fools fancy themselves as learned. In fact they are blind, and so they wander about in this world like the blind being led by the blind.

6. This passing to the other world is not visible to the ignorant. They are deluded by the illusion of wealth, and so they think, "This is the only world, there is no other." In this way they fall under my power over and over again.

7. There are many who hear about this, but still cannot comprehend it. Rare is the person who teaches it. Lucky is the person who hears it. Rare is the person who has understood it, and lucky is the person who has taught it.[12]

8. This matter cannot be understood when it is taught by an unqualified person. It has to be taught by the one who knows. There is no other way because the matter is subtle and beyond the realm of reason.

9. This subject cannot be understood by the explanations of an unqualified teacher. Yet, my child, it can be understood with the help of a proper teacher. Indeed, you are fixed on truth and so you have understood. How blessed we are to have a student like you, Naciketas!

[12] This verse is reminiscent of BG 2.29. In fact, there are many verses in this Upanishad which can be found in the BG verbatim or at least in similar form. This is one.

[13] There is an important concept behind this verse. The things of this world are material and therefore impermanent. This includes wealth. However, when these same impermanent material things are employed in a spiritual way, they can actually be used to attain what is permanent. Therefore, the bricks and ghee and wood that are in themselves impermanent material things become the means to attain the spiritual and permanent when they are used for a spiritual purpose.

[14] The word *deva* is literally a "shining one." Here it could refer to the individual soul (*jīvātmā*) or super soul (*paramātmā*).

[15] That is to say you are beyond death.

[16] The word is *padam* and it has multiple meanings, including "word," "a way," "a goal," or "a place." So this verse could be translated as "That word which all the Vedas declare..."

[Naciketas]
10. I know that wealth is impermanent, and I know that one cannot obtain the permanent with the impermanent. Yet I have built this *nāciketas* fire-altar using the things of impermanence to obtain what is permanent.[13]

[Death]
11. Naciketas, you are wise for you have understood that the fulfillment of desires is the foundation of this world, that the world constantly strives for security, and that all this has been praised as the highest thing–yet you have rejected it all.

12. Through inner contemplation, the wise finds within himself that shining one[14] who is primal, subtle, and hidden in the most secret place. In this way he rises above happiness and distress.

13. When a person of this world, a mortal, has heard and understood these teachings and is able to utilize this subtle doctrine, he rejoices because he has found the source of all happiness. That is you, Naciketas, and my home is open to you.[15]

[Naciketas]
14. Please tell me, O Death, what you see that is beyond *dharma* and *adharma*. Tell me what is beyond good and bad. Tell me what is beyond the past and the future.

[Death]
15. That goal[16] which all the Vedas proclaim, which all those who practice austerities speak about, and which men desire as

they live the religious life, that goal I will now declare unto you.[17] It is *om*!

16. This indeed is the imperishable[18] *brahma*. It is the highest,

---

[17] The last half of this verse matches BG 8.11.

[18] There are multiple ways to translate this verse. The word "imperishable" is a rendering of *akṣara*, which can also be "syllable." And so the verse may also be rendered as "This syllable (*om*) is *brahma*. This syllable is the supreme, and knowing this syllable one's desires are fulfilled."

[19] Presumably it is the incarnate individual self/soul that is being referred to here and in the following verse.

[20] This is essentially BG 2.20.

[21] Word for word this is BG 2.19.

[22] The expression is *dhātu-prasādāt*. *Dhātu* means "essence" or "essential part." *Prasāda* means "tranquility," but also "grace." So what is that essential part? Some take it as the mind and senses; others take it as God. In this way the translation can read "with the tranquility of the mind" or "through the grace of God." The idea of divine grace is the cornerstone of *bhakti*. The Shvetasvatara Upanishad develops this idea of divine grace in a verse that clearly mirrors the present verse: See ŚU 3.20, *tam akratum paśyati vīta-śoko dhātuḥ prasādān mahimānam īśam.*

[23] The word is *deva*, which is literally "a shining one" from the root *div*, "to shine." More commonly *deva* is translated as "a god."

[24] See MU 3.2.3. The words are *tanūṃ svām*. *Tanū* is body, form or self. *Svām* is one's own. The idea of divine grace is also implied in this verse. We have also seen previous evidence of this in this Upanishad. See 2.20 with the words *dhātu-prasāda.* Some commentators interpret this not as the grace of God, but as self-effort: Through self-effort the true nature of the *ātmā* is revealed.

and those who know this become fully satisfied.

17. It is the best support; it is the highest support. And those who understand this become fully satisfied.

18. This all-knowing One[19] is never born, nor does it ever die. It does not come from anywhere, nor does it become anything. Unborn, eternal, everlasting, this ancient one is not slain when the body is slain.[20]

19. If the slayer thinks he can kill or if the slain thinks he is slain, both do not understand, for neither can kill or be killed.[21]

20. This *ātmā,* which lays hidden in the heart of a being, is finer than the finest and greater than the greatest. One whose desires are subdued and whose mind and senses are tranquil[22] can see the majesty of this *ātmā* and so become released from sorrow.

21. Even though seated, this One travels afar. Even though laying down, It moves everywhere. Other than myself, who else is able to know this shining One[23] Who exists in perpetual joy.

22. The wise who see this great Lord, the all-pervading One, as the bodiless Lord within all bodies and the unchanging amongst the changing, cease from all suffering.

23. This Soul of All cannot be understood by teaching, nor by intellect, nor even by great learning. Only the person whom this Lord favors can understand. To such a person this Lord reveals Its true nature.[24]

24. In spite of great intellect, if one lacks peace or calmness of mind due to bad activities, one can never comprehend this Lord.[25]

25. Who is able to find that One for whom *brāhmaṇas* and *kṣatriyas* are mere food[26] and death is the sauce?

Here Ends the Second *Vallī*

---

[25] The word is *prajñāna,* which is wisdom or intellect or even cognizance.

[26] *Odana*, boiled rice.

[27] This is a description of two kinds of *ātmās*, the *jīvātmā* and the *paramātmā.* The *jīvātmā* is the individual soul which resides in the body along with mind and senses. Here it is described as *chāyā,* or shaded. The *paramātmā* is the higher soul, God, here described as *tapas,* or fiery. Both reside in the heart of the living being and both experience the ways of life in this world of action, the difference being that the *jīvātmā* is completely attached and enmeshed in the world of action, whereas the *paramātmā* is detached and just accompanies the individual soul during its sojourn in this world of action.

[28] The word is *guhā,* which is a cave and hiding place. In the context of the body, the heart is typically called the cave and the seat of the soul.

[29] The expression is *parame parārdhe* and it can be understood in many ways. *Parama* is "supreme" and *parārdhe* is a "distant place," so the expression can be read as a "supreme, distant place." I have glossed it as "that most subtle place."

[30] The word is *bhoktṛ,* and it means enjoyer. The *jīvātmā* is the individual soul which inhabits a body, complete with mind and senses. It is this soul who is the "enjoyer" in the sense of experiencer, both positive and negative, of the activities of the body, mind and senses. In later verses he is also called a honey-eater.

Third *Vallī*

1. Those learned in the ways of *brahma*, who maintain the five sacrificial fires and three times build the *nāciketas* altar, speak of two souls, the shaded and the light.[27] Together both have entered the cave of the heart,[28] that most subtle place,[29] and enjoy the ways of action in this world.

2. May we master the *nāciketas* sacrifice, which is the bridge for those who sacrifice and who desire to cross to that far off shore of fearlessness in the realm of the imperishable supreme *brahma*.

3-4. The *ātmā* is the owner of the chariot; the body is the chariot. The intellect is the chariot driver; the mind is the reins. The senses are the horses; the sense objects are the paths. The one who is connected to the body, its senses and its mind is the enjoyer.[30] This has been declared by the wise.

5-6. When a person lacks understanding and self-discipline, the mind is constantly disturbed, and the senses are also out of control. This is like a chariot pulled by untrained horses. On the other hand, if a person has understanding and self-discipline, the mind is restrained and so the senses are also under control. This is like a chariot pulled by trained horses.

7-8. When a person lacks understanding and self-discipline, he becomes foolish and impure. Such a person can never reach the

[31] The word is *padam,* which literally means foot or step, but also a place or destination.

[32] The words here are *tad viṣṇoḥ paramaṃ padam.* The identical words are used in RV 1.22.20a, and similar words are found in RV 1.154.5d *(viṣṇoḥ pade parame).* Both can be translated as "the supreme abode of Viṣṇu." In this case, of course, *viṣṇoḥ, "of Viṣṇu,"* is taken as the deity Viṣṇu. In my translation above, I take the word *viṣṇu* not as the name of the deity, but in a universal sense, as "the All-Pervading One." The word *viṣṇu* is derived from *viś,* meaning "to enter;" so *viṣṇu* becomes the one who enters all things, hence "all-pervading." So the question arises, is the Upanishad referring to the particular or the universal? In this Upanishad there is no reference to any specific deity until suddenly this reference appears. For this reason, I have opted for the universal translation as opposed to a specific translation.

[33] Here the word used is *avyakta*, "un-manifest." The words used in this verse suggest the origins of the later Sānkhya philosophy. According to Sānkhya, this manifest world is thought to have burst forth and evolved from a primordial "soup," the great un-manifest, *avyakta.* This *avyakta* is also called *pradhāna* or *prakriti* and is thought to be female. Next to this *avyakta* is another, superior principle called *puruṣa.* The word *puruṣa* is literally "man" and it is naturally thought to be male. *Puruṣa* "glances" over at *avyakta* and creation initiates. From this primordial *puruṣa, ātmā* "breaks off" and enters into *prakriti* to become the living beings in this world.

[34] Later theistic schools often cite this reference to *puruṣa* as the ultimate goal in support of the idea that God is ultimately personal. In the Vaishnavite schools, this *puruṣa* is identified with Vishnu and His *avatāras* Rama and Krishna.

[35] These terms—knowledge-self, great-self, peaceful-self—can be taken as the intellectual self, the self that feels identity, and the meditative self, respectively. In other words, there is a hierarchy of control: that lower elements are controlled by higher elements. The peaceful self is a reference to the peace one finds by turning inward.

final destination.[31] Instead, he falls back into the cycle of birth and death. On the other hand, a person who possesses understanding and self-discipline becomes mindful and pure. Such a person reaches the final destination and becomes freed from the cycle of birth and death.

9. When a person's disciplined intellect is the chariot driver and the controlled mind is the reins, he reaches the end of his journey, the supreme place of the All-Pervading One.[32]

10. The sense objects are superior to the senses. The mind is superior to the sense objects. Superior to the mind is the intellect. But highest of all is that great *ātmā*.

11. Yet the great un-manifest[33] is superior even to this *ātmā*. Higher still is the *puruṣa*. Indeed, nothing is higher than *puruṣa*, for it is the ultimate goal.[34]

12. Even though this *ātmā* exists within all living beings, it is hidden and so cannot be easily perceived. Yet it can be perceived by learned ones with discerning intellects.

13. The wise must control mind and speech. Mind and speech must be controlled by the knowledge-self. The knowledge-self should be controlled by the great-self. The great-self should be controlled by the peaceful-self.[35]

14. Arise! Awaken! Understand the blessings you have received! A razor's edge is hard to cross, and so is this path; yet the

learned have explained the path for you.

15. It is silent. It cannot be touched. It has no form. It is imperishable. It has no taste or odor. It is without beginning. It has no end and it is beyond all things. And when you have understood this you can escape the jaws of death!

16. The wise, who recite this ancient story of Naciketas that was originally told by Yama, the god of death himself, rejoice in the realm of *brahma*.

17. When one hears of this supreme secret in the assembly of *brāhmanas* or at the time of the rites for the dead, the path to immortality opens. Indeed, the path to immortality opens wide.

Here Ends the Third *Vallī*

---

[36] Literally, "pierced the apertures of the body."

[37] It is the *ātmā* that brings consciousness into the body.

[38] Even though the *ātmā* is not visible in the body, it is the source of consciousness and all things are known to it.

[39] Verse 3.1 of this Upanishad talks about two forms of *ātmā,* which both dwell within the body. One is called light and the other is called shadow. In later forms of Hinduism these two souls are referred to as *jīvātmā* and *paramātmā*, the ordinary soul and the super-soul, so to speak. In this verse that shadow *ātmā*, the ordinary soul, is called a honey-eater. That means he is the enjoyer in this world. Moving from one lifetime to another, from one species to another, this individual soul moves about "tasting" the pleasures of this world. The *paramātmā* or super soul, on the other hand, (continued page 114)

Fourth *Vallī*

1. At the time of creation, Svayambhu, the creator, fashioned the senses[36] in such a way that they look outward. People therefore naturally look outward. But those who seek immortality have learned to search within, and so they use the eye of introspection to see the immortal *ātmā*.

2. Common folk seek to fulfill their desires in the outer world. They fail to see the noose of death that is spread before them. But the learned, who understand the immortal, never pursue eternal things amongst the impermanent things of this world.

3. It is through *ātmā* alone that one experiences form, taste, scent, sound, and touch.[37] What is there that remains to be known?[38] This, indeed, is that.

4. It is through the *ātmā* alone that one experiences both the dream world and the wakened world. And because the wise know this great and all-pervading *ātmā,* they are free of suffering in this world.

5. When a person knows the honey-eater, the living being who lives within the body, that Lord of past and future never hides away from him.[39] This, indeed, is that.

6. This one who existed before heat, who existed before water, who has entered that secret place of the heart, remains there see-

ing through the eyes of beings. This, indeed, is that.

7. That divine energy, *aditi*, who manifests through breath enters the hidden place in the heart of beings and remains there. This, indeed, is that.

8. Fire, hidden within kindling wood, which is protected and nurtured like an embryo within the womb of a woman, should be evoked each day by those who are awake and who perform the sacred fire rites. This, indeed, is that.

9. From where the sun rises and to where it sets, all the divinities reside within these boundaries. Who can cross this limit? This, indeed, is that.

---

is the form of God in this world who accompanies this ordinary soul throughout its travels from one birth to another through various species. In fact, these two forms of *ātmā* are the same although they appear to be different. This is the meaning of the expression that is repeated here, "This, indeed, is that." The key point is this: Know one and you can know the other. If one can come to know the ordinary *ātmā*, the *jīvātmā*, then one can know the other *ātmā*, the *paramātmā*.

[40] This is a recurring theme of the Upanishads: This and that are the same. See BU 2.3.1 and 5.1.1.

[41] This is a reference to either the *paramātmā or the jīvātmā.*

[42] This is a reference to the body. Other places call this the city of nine gates.

[43] A person who is liberated even while residing in a physical body is called *jīvan-mukta*. Such a person has no need to be reborn.

10. What is here is there, and what is there is here. The one who sees a difference between here and there goes from death to death.[40]

11. There is no difference. This needs to be realized in the mind. The one who sees a difference goes from death to death.

12. There is a Person the size of a thumb situated in the middle of the heart.[41] He is the Lord of what has been and what will be. No one hides from him. This, indeed, is that.

13. This Person the size of a thumb is like a flame without smoke. He is the Lord of what has been and what will be. He is the same today and the same tomorrow. This, indeed, is that.

14. As rainwater falling in the mountains flows through rough terrain and so dissipates, so the vision of a person who sees things as separate flows in all directions.

15. As pure water, O Gautama, poured into pure water remains unchanged, so does the *ātmā* of the discerning sage.

Here Ends the Fourth *Vallī*

Fifth *Vallī*

1. There is a city of eleven gates[42] wherein the unborn and pure soul comes to reside. The learned man who understands the nature of *ātmā* has no lamentation for he has won deliverance.[43]

Indeed, he is liberated. This, indeed, is that.

2. This *ātmā* is the swan who dwells in the heavens.[44] He is the light in the sky. He is the priest sitting at the altar. He is the guest dwelling in the house. He resides in men, in truth, and in the sky. He is born in water, he is born in the earth, he is born in

---

[44] That is to say, the sun.

[45] The word is *prāṇa*.

[46] The word is *apāna*.

[47] The word is *deva*, which is generally translated as "god," but, as we have seen in other places in the Upanishads, often refers to the senses of the body.

[48] The word is *vāmana*. It also means dwarf. This is the *paramātmā* mentioned above, who resides in the heart and who measures the size of a thumb.

[49] "Fixed forms" means trees, etc.

[50] The words are *karma* and *śruta*, actions and hearing.

[51] The word *puruṣa* means "person." In this case this *puruṣa* could be the individual soul, *jīvātmā*, or the super-soul, *paramātmā*. All throughout this section of the Upanishads we see the expression *etad vai tat,* "this, indeed, is that," which suggests the relationship between the individual soul and this super-soul. They are identical. And yet we also see the word *bahi,* meaning "outside" or "distinct," used in the following two verses, suggesting that the two are separate. So there is a subtle relationship between the two. They are identical and they are distinct. This has led to the development of the three basic Vedantic theologies: the two are absolutely identical (*advaita*), the two are absolutely distinct (*dvaita*), or the two are both identical and distinct simultaneously (*dvaitādvaita*).

[52] This can also be read as the fire of digestion.

sacred tradition, and he is born in rock. He is power. He is divine law.

3. He causes the in-breath[45] to rise upwards and the out-breath[46] to move downwards. All the senses[47] venerate this adorable one[48] who sits in the middle.

4. When the soul, which is situated within the body, is released from that body, what is there that remains? This, indeed, is that.

5. No mortal being lives solely by the in-breath or the out-breath, but on another who is the support of these two breaths.

6. So now I shall tell you about this eternal and hidden *brahma* and what happens to the soul after death, O Gautama.

7. Amongst those souls destined for embodiment, some enter wombs and others enter fixed forms.[49] All this occurs according to their activities and learning.[50]

8. Amongst those who sleep there is the *puruṣa,*[51] who is awake and who creates an endless chain of desires. This *puruṣa* is bright. It is *brahma* and it is immortal. All these worlds rest on this *brahma*. There is nothing beyond this. This, indeed, is that.

9. As fire[52] exists in this world as one, it takes different forms according to whatever it burns. So the one *ātmā*, which is the inner soul of all beings, assumes different forms according to whatever it enters, and yet it remains distinct.

10. As the air[53] exists as one, it takes different forms according to wherever it goes. So the one *ātmā*, which is the inner soul of all beings, takes on different forms according to whatever it enters, and yet it remains distinct.

11. As the sun is the eye of all the worlds and yet is never affected by the external defects of vision, so the one *ātmā*, who is the inner soul of all beings, is never affected by the outer sufferings of the world.

12. There is a controller, who is the inner soul of all beings and who manifests his single form in diverse ways. The wise, who can recognize this controller within themselves, find everlasting joy. Others do not.

---

[53] This can also be read as the air of breath.

[54] *nityo nityānāṃ cetanaś cetanānām.* This is a well-known expression stating that the *puruṣa* is the prime constant and the prime intelligence amongst all things constant and intelligent.

[55] This verse is similar to BG 15.6.

[56] The simile of the world as an inverted fig tree is found is other Upanishads (see MuU 2.2.10 and SU 6.14) as well as in the Gita (BG 15.1-3).

[57] *etad vai tat,* "this truly is that," is repeated throughout this chapter. It shows the identification of the *jivātmā* and the *paramātmā*. Know this and you know that.

[58] The word used here is *prāṇe*, literally "on breath." *Prāṇa* is one of those words open to a wide range of interpretation.

[59] Literally, a "great fear," *mahad-bhayam.*

13. This One is the chief constant amongst all things constant.[54] It is the intelligence of the intelligent, the One amongst the many, and the One who fulfills desires. Learned persons who can perceive this One within themselves are forever at peace. But not others.

14. "This is that!" In this way the learned experience indescribable joy. How can I also come to know this? Does it shine on its own or does it shine by reflection?

15. In that place there is no need for sunlight, nor moonlight, nor even the light of stars. Lightning does not shine there, nor even the light of fire. It alone shines and all things reflect the light of this One.[55]

Here Ends the Fifth *Vallī*

Sixth *Vallī*

1. There is an eternal fig tree with its roots upward and its branches downward.[56] There is *brahma.* It is luminous. It is immortal, and all these worlds rest on it. There is nothing beyond this. This truly is that.[57]

2. Whatever exists in this animate world has been created and moves because of *brahma.*[58] It is a great force,[59] terrible like a raised thunderbolt. Those who understand this become immortal.

3. Out of fear of this force fire burns, the sun shines, and storms, the wind, and even death itself move about in this world.

4. As much as one is able to understand this before the body

---

[60] This is a difficult verse and, left alone, it makes little sense. Therefore, commentators suggest modifications to the verse. Here, what I have rendered as "as much as" is *cet*, "if." To the degree one is able to perceive *brahma* in one's current lifetime, this determines one's rebirth status. Some commentators add a *na* to the verse, meaning if one does **not** understand *brahma* in this lifetime, one takes rebirth. Other commentators change "in these worlds" to "in the worlds of heaven."

[61] The word is *ātmā*, so the meaning could be body or soul or self, etc. "As in a mirror, so in the body, so in the mind, so in the intellect... ."

[62] The meaning is obscure, but the context suggests different degrees of clarity perceiving the *ātmā* and the *paramātmā.*

[63] Literally, the words are *avyaktam uttamam*, "highest unmanifest." The meaning is obscure.

[64] Literally, the word *puruṣa* means person.

[65] See ŚU 4.20 a and b.

[66] See ŚU 3.13 c and d, and 4.17 c and d.

[67] The expression is *indriya-dhāraṇa,* literally "holding the senses."

[68] *Prabhavāpyayau,* "the coming into being as well as the ceasing to be." This expression is obscure. Some commentators say that yoga has both a good side and a dangerous side. Others say it means that when one begins the process of yoga there is both the destruction of bad qualities and the appearance of good qualities.

perishes, one accordingly takes birth in these worlds.[60]

5. As in a mirror, so in the *ātmā.*[61] As in dreams, so in the worlds of the ancestors. As in water, so in the world of the Gandharvas. As in dark and light, so in the world of Brahmā.[62]

6. The wise, understanding the distinct nature of the senses—that they belong to the body and not the soul—cease to grieve.

7. The mind is superior to the senses; higher than the mind is the intellect. Higher still is the self, and above even the self is the great unmanifest, *brahma.*[63]

8. But highest of all, beyond the unmanifest, is the all-pervading and invisible *Puruṣa.*[64] One who knows this *Puruṣa* attains immortality.

9. The form of this *Puruṣa* is beyond sight. He cannot be seen with the eye.[65] However, the heart, the intellect and the mind can be used to partially conceive of this *Puruṣa*. Those who understand this can attain immortality.[66]

10-11. When the five knowledge-gathering senses, along with the mind and intellect, have become still, one has reached the supreme state of yoga. As one gains control over the senses[67] and fixes the mind, one becomes completely free of distraction. This is yoga and it is both a coming and a going.[68]

12. Not through speech, not through thought, and not even through sight can He be apprehended. Only in affirming "He is!"[69] can He be understood. How else can He be known?

13. Between the two ways[70] of understanding this *Puruṣa,* one positive and the other negative, the positive affirmation "He is!" is the best way to know the true nature of *Puruṣa.*

14. When the desires of the heart are completely removed, the mortal becomes immortal and one can attain *brahma.*

15. When the knots of the heart that bind one to this world are

---

[69] The Sanskrit is *astīti,* "He is!" I take this as a "nonverbal" affirmation, and by this I mean an opening of the heart to the possibility of divinity, a leap of faith if you will, free of doubt or any form of intellectual filtering.

[70] The Sanskrit says *ubhayoḥ,* "between the two." There is, however, no indication of what the two are. Previously the Brihad Aranyaka and the Chandogya Upanishads had introduced the notion of *apoha,* understanding what is beyond comprehension in negative terms: *neti, neti,* not this, not this. Here a positive approach is taken: *asti, asti,* He is, He is. Another understanding of what the two may be is the idea of *saguna brahma* and *nirguna brahma, brahma* with qualities and *brahma* without qualities. The notion of *puruṣa* is *brahma* as a person, with qualities. This is *saguna brahma.*

[71] In the language of *kundalini-yoga,* this pathway is called *suṣumṇā,* and the crown of the head is called *brahma-randhra.*

[72] This verse is also found in CU 8.6.6, KauU 4.19 and BU 4.2.3.

split open, the mortal becomes immortal. This is the teaching.

16. There are a hundred and one pathways leading from the heart. One goes directly to the crown of the head.[71] The person who follows this pathway attains immortality. All the other pathways lead to rebirth.[72]

17. This *puruṣa,* the size of a thumb, resides deep in the heart. One should extract this *puruṣa* from the body with determination, like the stalk is extracted from a reed. This *puruṣa* is immortal and bright. Indeed, He is immortal and bright!

[Narrator]
18. Naciketas thus heard these teachings spoken by Yama, including the rules of yoga. As a result, he became free from passion and death and attained *brahma*. In this way, others who hear these teachings may also attain *brahma*!

Here Ends the Sixth *Vallī*
Here Ends the Katha Upanishad

6

Isha Upanishad

Introduction to

Isha Upanishad

The Isha Upanishad, like the Kena Upanishad, gets its name from its first word, *īśā* ("by a Lord"). It forms the fortieth chapter of the Vajasaneyi Samhita of the White Yajurveda. Of all the Upanishads, the Isha Upanishad is the most theistic and devotional. It is also one of the shortest Upanishads with just 18 verses, and yet, due to its devotional leanings, has had the greatest influence on the later traditions. The doctrines and ideas suggest that it belongs broadly to the time and milieu that produced other similar Upanishads with a strong theistic and devotional tendency, such as the SU, MuU, and, to a somewhat lesser extent, the KaU.

Ishopanishad

1. Whatever exists in this moving world is pervaded[1] by a Lord.[2] You may enjoy[3] this world, but only in a renounced way.[4] Never covet the wealth of another.

2. Acting in this way, you may aspire to live a hundred years.

---

[1] "Is pervaded" is a translation of *āvāsyam,* which is literally "covered" or "enveloped."

[2] Even though this Upanishad is largely regarded as a devotional work, no specific deity is mentioned as the Lord. "By a Lord" (*īśā*) is literally "by a controlling force." That no specific deity is mentioned means that the text can be interpreted in either a universal or a specific way. Some commentators say the Lord is the *ātmā;* others say it means the Lord of sacrifice, Vishnu; and still others take it as some higher power, a force.

[3] "You may enjoy" (*bhuñjīthā*) is derived from the verbal root *bhuj,* which means to enjoy, to eat, to consume, or to possess. Here the Upanishad acknowledges that the living beings in this world are "enjoyers," that they have a right to enjoy this world, but only in a specific way, noted as *tena tyaktena,* in a renounced way. See fn below.

[4] "In a renounced way" is from *tena tyaktena,* which is literally "through renunciation." This evokes the idea of stewardship—that there is a Lord, be it a particular deity or some higher force, which owns and governs this physical world. The beings of this world do not own or control the things of this world. Given that recognition, the higher beings of this world have the obligation to steward or care for this world without a sense of ownership. Many traditional commentators interpret this expression, *tena tyaktena bhuñjīthā,* as "you must protect yourself through renunciation."

For such action does not bind[5] a person, while other actions do.

3. Indeed there are hellish worlds,[6] places of utter darkness. Those who deny the soul[7] proceed to them after departing this world.[8]

4. There is an immovable One,[9] quicker than the mind, whom even the gods[10] cannot touch. Though remaining still, It rushes

---

[5] "For such action does not bind" (*na karma lipyate*) is literally "action does not stain." This means that actions undertaken with detachment and without a sense of ownership do not bind the performer. Actions performed without this understanding do bind the performer.

[6] "Hellish worlds" (*asuryā 'nāma te lokā*) is literally "places fit for the demoniac." Some commentators interpret this as births in lower forms of life, such as trees, etc. Others says it means places without happiness. A variant reading is *asūryā,* sunless worlds.

[7] "Deny the soul" (*ātma-hana*) is literally "kill the *ātmā.*" Given that the *ātmā*, by very definition, cannot be killed, we have glossed this as "deny the soul." Emerging around the time of this Upanishad there were the Buddhist and Jaina doctrines of *anātmā*, no soul. One wonders whether *ātma-hana* is a reference to these Buddhist and Jaina doctrines.

[8] This verse is similar to BU 4.4.11: "Joyless are those worlds of dense darkness. Persons who live in ignorance and who are unconscious enter these worlds after death."

[9] "There is an immovable One:" Some commentators interpret the one (*ekam*) as the *ātmā,* the all encompassing single Soul. Others takes it as Vishnu, the Lord of Sacrifice. That no deity is ever named specifically in this Upanishad is a tribute to the universal nature of this Upanishad in spite of it being the most theistic of all the Upanishads.

ahead. Its heat and breath[11] generate action[12] within its being.

5. It moves. It moves not.[13] It is far. It is near. It is within all things and yet It exists outside of all things.[14]

6. Indeed, the one who sees this Lord within all beings and all beings within this Lord[15] is not beset by fear.[16]

7. Where is the delusion or sorrow for the person who sees this oneness[17] and who understands how this Lord has become all beings?

---

[10] "The gods" (*deva˙*) is here interpreted by many commentators to be the senses of the body, "the shining ones." The word *deva* is derived from the root *div*, to shine. The English word divine is similarly from *div*.

[11] "Heat and breath" (*mātariśvan*) are literally the fire and wind gods.

[12] "Action" (*apa*) may also refer to primordial waters.

[13] "It moves. It moves not" (*tad ejati tan naijati*): The verbal root is *ej,* meaning to move, shake or tremble. Most commentators take this as movement in general. Some take it as fear.

[14] Compare this verse to BG 13.15. "It exists both within all things as well as outside of all things. It is moving as well as unmoving; and due to its subtle nature, it is unknowable. It is both distant and yet very near." This verse raises the idea that the divine is both immanent and transcendent.

[15] Here the use of "Lord" is a translation of "*ātmā*."

[16] "Is not beset by fear" (*na vijugupsate*) is literally "does not hide away." Some take it as "does not despise anyone." Compare this verse to BG 6.30: "For one who sees Me everywhere and who sees all things in Me, I am never lost, nor is that one ever lost to Me."

[17] "Oneness" is a translation of "*ekatvam*."

8. This Lord is all pervading, radiant, bodiless, unhurt, without sinews, pure, and untouched by evil. He is the seer, the wise one, and the self-existent governing principle. From the beginning He has rightly apportioned the objects of the world.

9. Those who are intent upon *avidyā* enter blinding darkness. But those who delight in *vidyā* enter an even greater darkness.[18]

10. One result arises from *vidyā* and another result arises from *avidyā*. We have learned this from the wise.[19]

---

[18] Verses 9 through 11 form a section, and verses 12 through 14 form a separate but similar section. Verse 9 is identical with BU 4.4.10. Both these sections are obscure, and commentators over the millennia have struggled to come up with meaning. Literally, *vidyā* is knowledge and *avidyā* is the opposite, non-knowledge or ignorance. So in this verse, if we translate *avidyā* as ignorance, it then makes reasonable sense to translate the first part as "Those who are intent upon **ignorance** enter blinding darkness." But to translate the second half as: "But those who delight in **knowledge** enter an even greater darkness" makes no sense. How can knowledge lead to an even worst situation than ignorance? This problem forces the commentator to come up with an explanation. One explanation is to say that the text is corrupt; another is to change the meaning of *avidyā* and *vidyā*. Instead of ignorance and knowledge we see "ritual knowledge" and "knowledge of gods," "imminence and transcendence," "being and non-being," etc. One that I prefer is "material knowledge" and "spiritual knowledge"—that is, to contrast knowledge of practical things, like architecture, medicine, plumbing, etc., with knowledge of metaphysical things, like the soul and God.

11. One who possesses both *avidyā* and *vidyā,* with *avidyā* transcends death and with *vidyā* attains immortality.[20]

12. Those who see the world as *asaṃbhūti* enter blinding darkness. But those who delight in seeing the world as *saṃbhūti* enter an even greater darkness.[21]

Regardless of how we translate *vidyā* and *avidyā,* we must understand that they are opposites. And so, according to this Upanishad, both sides of life, the spiritual and the material, need to be utilized to achieve the successful life. What comprises complete knowledge, therefore, is the combination of both *vidyā* and *avidyā*. To regard practical knowledge as a form of ignorance or somehow inferior is wrong, and to think that one can survive on spiritual knowledge alone is also wrong. Spiritual knowledge understood as knowledge of the soul and God is incomplete; practical knowledge understood as knowledge of hygiene, architecture, medicine, etc., is also important. Even a *yogī,* a monk, needs a place to live, food, protection and hygiene, etc., all things derived from *avidyā*, practical knowledge.

[19] The meaning is that the Supreme cannot be attained by either *vidyā* or *avidyā* alone. The following verse says that they must be applied together.

[20] This verse confirms that both *avidyā* and *vidyā*—that is to say both practical knowledge and spiritual knowledge—are necessary for true spiritual development.

[21] Literally, *sambhūti* means birth, creation, production, existence, etc., and so *asambhūti* is the opposite: destruction, dissolution, non-existence, etc. Like *vidyā* and *avidyā,* the terms are opposites and so also show that the successful life arises from the combination of both.

13. One result arises from *asaṃbhūti* and another result arises from *saṃbhūti*. We have learned this from the wise.[22]

14. One who understands the world both in terms of *saṃbhūti* and *asaṃbhūti,* with *asaṃbhūti* crosses death and with *saṃbhūti* attains immortality.[23]

15. O Sustainer of the Universe,[24] your glowing radiance[25] covers your face of truth. O God of Light, I am a lover of truth. I wish to see you now. Please reveal yourself.[26]

---

[22] In this verse the terms have shifted from *asambhūti* and *sambhūti* to *asambhava* and *sambhava. Asambhava* and *sambhava* are the equivalent of *asambhūti* and *sambhūti.*

[23] As in verse 10, the Supreme cannot be attained by one or the other, but only in combination. How does an understanding of the destructive principle help overcome death? Commentators say it leads to the destruction of one's vices and other faults that force one to be continually reborn into this world.

[24] "O Sustainer of the Universe" is a translation of Pushan, a Vedic deity identified with the sun and therefore the surveyor of all things. This deity is also the conductor on journeys to the next world.

[25] "Glowing radiance" (*hiraṇmayena pātreṇa*) is literally "by a golden vessel." Some commentators interpret this as the sun.

[26] Verses 15 to 18 are to be recited at the time of death or during a funeral ceremony. These verses first appear in BU 5.15.

16. O Sustainer, Sole Seer, Controller, O Sun, O Creative Principle,[27] disperse your glaring radiance, gather together your light. I wish to behold your most wonderful form, that most distant person of which I am a part.[28]

17. O Supreme,[29] my breath to the immortal wind, this body to ashes.

O Guiding Intelligence, remember all that I have done. O Grand Design,[30] remember my deeds. Do not forget me.

18. O Agni,[31] lead me to prosperity. You alone know the way. Forgive my sins. [32] To you I offer unlimited prayer.

Here Ends the Isha Upanishad

---

[27] "O Creative Principle" is literally "descendent of Prajapati" (*prājāpatya*).,

[28] "That most distant person of which I am a part" (*yo 'sāv asau puruṣa˙ so 'ham asmi*) is literally "that yonder person, he I am."'

[29] "O Supreme" is a gloss on "*Om*."

[30] "O Guiding Intelligence" and "O Grand Design" are both translations of *kratu*, which is literally plan, design, intelligence, enlightenment, etc.

[31] Agni is the fire deity. Since the body is cremated, the prayer is to God as fire.

[32] "Forgive my sins" (*yuyodhy asmaj juhurāṇam*) is literally "overcome" or "battle our crooked ways."

7

Shvetashvatara Upanishad

Introduction to
Shvetashvatara Upanishad

The Shvetashvatara Upanishad is part of the Black Yajurveda and is so named after its teacher, Shvetashvatara mentioned at the end. It contains 113 verses arranged into six chapters. Like most things of ancient India, its date of composition is hard to pinpoint, but there is a general consensus that the Shvetashvatara Upanishad was compiled around the second or third century BCE. Regardless of its overall dating, the Shvetashvatara Upanishad is a later work compared to the other Upanishads. We say this because of the theistic nature of the Upanishad and its drift away from the Vedic *yajña* as the primary religious activity. The earliest Upanishads, such as the Brihad Aranyaka and the Chandogya, are highly focused on the Vedic *yajña*, and even though they have a lot of discussion on the nature of *brahma*, *ātmā* and *prāṇa*, they are wholly non-theistic, and certainly no specific deity is named as the "face" of *brahma*. Yet, over time we see a drifting away from the Vedic *yajña* as the main religious activity and its gradual replacement with theism and *bhakti*. The Isha Upanishad, for example, expresses strong theis-

---

[1] The words *kiṃ karanaṃ brahma* might also mean "What is the cause? What is *brahma*?" or "Is the cause *brahma*?" or "Is *brahma* the cause?" or even "What sort of a cause is *brahma*?"

[2] If *ātmā* were the ultimate cause, it seems unlikely that it would create a universe that would create its own suffering. Therefore, *ātmā* cannot be the ultimate cause.

tic tendencies, but without the mention of a specific deity. Instead, there is mention of a supreme deity in a generic way, as *īśa*, the Controller. In just a few verses from its third *adhyāya* this Shvetashvatara Upanishad goes one step further and speaks of a Most Terrible One, Rudra, a precursor to Shiva, as the face of *brahma*. It even includes prayers to this Terrible One for protection and help. The Upanishads in general do not mention any specific deity as the face of *brahma*. This gives them a universal appeal. The theistic nature and the near mention of a particular deity puts this Upanishad on par with the Bhagavad Gita, which has a later chronology, and which is even more theistic and devotional, extolling Krishna as the supreme deity. In fact, many verses of the Gita are taken right out of this Shvetashvatara and the Katha Upanishads.

First *Adhyāya*

Students of *brahma* ask:

1-2. What is the cause? Is it *brahma*?[1] From what source do beings come? By what do they live? On what are they founded? Is there a controlling force whereby beings live in their different conditions of pleasure and pain? Is time the cause? Is it inherent nature? Is fate or mere chance the cause? Do beings arise simply from the union of male and female? Or is it a combination of these? Is *ātmā*, the individual soul, the cause? Yet *ātmā* itself has little control over its own pleasure and pain.[2] O knowers of *brahma*, please explain this to us.

3. All these causes—from time to *ātmā*—are governed by a Controller.[3] Those who practice the yoga of meditation can see this Controller hidden by its divine power within all things.

4. We conceive of the universe as a great wheel with one rim, three tires, and sixteen end parts. Within this wheel are fifty

---

[3] The words are *devātma-śaktim,* literally "divine self-power."

[4] Both this verse and the following verse are based on *sānkhya* philosophy. Literally, the word *sānkhya* means enumeration and it refers to the process of "counting": that is to say, analyzing the constituents of matter. This is basically what modern science does. In the *Sankhya Karika*, a main work of the Sankhya School, the constituents of matter are enumerated and analyzed. It is not clear which came first, this Shvetashvatara Upanishad or the Sankhya system, but, regardless, the process is similar. It is enumeration. Here it is unclear exactly as to what all these numbers and divisions actually refer. Commentators are not in agreement. Even the terms "wheel" and "river" are not directly stated in the text. Instead, they are implied by the context and adjectives used. A guess as to what each element refers to is as follows: The one rim is the *prakriti* of *sānkhya* philosophy, primordial matter. The three tires are the three *guna: sattva*, *rajas* and *tamas*, goodness, passion and darkness. The sixteen end parts are the five basic elements of matter—earth, water, fire, air and space—the five organs of perception, the five organs of action, and the mind. The fifty spokes and twenty counter spokes are the various elements that incite action. The six sets of eight are: (1) the eight elements of matter: earth, water, fire, air, space, mind, intellect, identity; (2) eight elements of the body: outer skin, inner skin, blood, flesh, fat, bone, marrow, and semen; (3) eight yogic powers: the power to become extremely small, extremely large, or extremely light, power to obtain anything, total

spokes and twenty counter spokes. This universe has six sets of eight along with an enchantment which is like a noose with many forms that deludes beings in two ways.[4]

5. We conceive of the universe as a river with five streams whose waters are from five sources, raging and ever-changing. The waves of this river are the five breaths,[5] whose foundation is the five perceptions. There are five whirlpools which create a flood of fivefold miseries and which divides itself in fifty ways with five sections.[6]

---

freedom of will, power to subdue all to one's will, lordship, and power of suppressing desire; (4) eight dispositions: righteousness and unrighteousness, knowledge and ignorance, detachment and non-detachment, superhuman power and lack of such power; (5) eight divine beings: Brahmā, Prajāpati, Devas, Gandharvas, Yaksas, Raksasas, Ancestors, and Pisacas; (6) eight virtues: compassion, forbearance, lack of envy, purity, ease, generosity, auspiciousness, and absence of desire. The noose is desire, and the two ways are good and bad actions.

[5] There are five "breaths" called *prāṇas,* and they include the incoming breath, the outgoing breath, the held breath, the circulatory system and the digestive system.

[6] The word used here is *srotas,* which is generally translated as a stream, but it can also be used for the senses. So the five rivers are the five senses. Another interpretation is the five streams are the mind, so that the mind is "fed" by five streams of perception from the five senses. The five sources are the five sense objects. The five perceptions are five perceptions arising from the five senses. The five whirlpools are the sense objects. The five miseries are the miseries associated with being in the womb and the miseries of delivery, sickness, old age and death. The "fifty ways with five sections" is obscure.

6. On this wheel of *brahma* a swan wanders.[7] This great wheel is the foundation for all beings and the source of their livelihood. This swan is blessed when it comes to understand the difference between the soul and the body. At that time the door to immortality opens.[8]

7. This supreme *brahma,* celebrated in the Upanishads, contains three constituents.[9] It is the imperishable substratum of all things. The knowers of *brahma,* who can discern this, become absorbed and devoted to this *brahma* and so become free of the womb.[10]

---

[7] This swan is the living being and the wheel is this phenomenal world.

[8] Here the words are *pṛthag-ātmānaṃ preritāram.* The word *pṛthak* is separateness or difference; *ātmānam* may have multiple meanings, including body, mind or soul; and *preritāram* refers to the one who incites action. So the question is who or what is the *ātmā* and who is the *preritā*, the inciter? Here the *ātmā* is taken as the body and the *preritā* is the individual soul. So understanding the difference between the body and the soul is the first step towards immortality. Another rendering could be to take *ātmā* as the individual soul and *preritā* as the super-soul (*paramātmā*). And so understanding the difference between the individual soul and the super-soul is the first step towards immortality. This would be a *dvaita* interpretation. But then there are the *advaita* commentators, who say there is an implied negative in this verse and so it means when one gives up seeing the distinction between the two, the door to immortality opens.

[9] God, the soul and matter. See fn. below.

[10] That is to say, free from rebirth.

[11] The three are God (*īś*), the soul (*ātmā*), and material nature (*prakṛti*). Both God and the soul are considered male, while material nature is

8. There is a Lord who supports this universe in all its parts, both seen and unseen, animate and inanimate. There is the individual soul, who is not the supreme Lord, but who sees himself as the enjoyer of this world and so becomes entangled. Only when this individual soul comes to understand this Lord can he be freed from his entanglements.

9. In this world are two males, both eternal, one omniscient and the other not. One is a controller and the other is not. There is also an eternal female, who connects these two males with the objects of enjoyment. This *ātmā* is limitless and assumes unlimited forms. He performs no action. When one finds these three,[11] one secures *brahma.*

10. Matter is perishable, whereas Spirit[12] is permanent and eternal. This one God rules both matter and spirit. Through meditation and worship of this Lord, and in seeking this Lord's nature, the illusion arising from matter can be mitigated.

---

considered female. When the *ātmā* mixes with material nature, it is called *jīvātmā,* a living being. When God interacts with material nature, it is called *paramātmā,* the super-soul. Material nature is considered the "playground" for both the *ātmā* and the *paramātmā.* While in this playground the *paramātmā* is a Lord or controller; the *jīvātmā,* on the other hand, is not. Consequently, the *jīvātmā* becomes entangled within this playground. Disentangling the *jīvātmā* from *prakṛti* is the objective of these teachings.

[12] The word is *hara,* which in later Hinduism is a name for Shiva, "one who removes." In this case, however, *hara* refers to either the *jīvātmā* or the *paramātmā;* hence the translation "spirit."

11. Through knowing this God, the fetters that bind can be cut, and birth and death can be stopped. In this way suffering ends. By meditation on Him one obtains a third state, control over one's destiny,[13] and in the absolute[14] one's desires are fulfilled upon the dissolution of this body.

12. There is an eternal essence that exists within our body,[15] and it can be known. Once known, what more is there? When one understands the enjoyer, the enjoyed and the overseer, one has understood the three manifestations of *brahma* in this world. All of this has been declared.

13. Just because one cannot see the fire that lays dormant within wood does not mean fire does not exist. It can be repeatedly brought out using a fire drill. So by using the sound *om* as if it was a fire drill, both the soul and the super-soul can be made

---

[13] Here the word is *viśvaiśvarya,* which I have taken as *viśva-aiśvarya*, "universal control."

[14] The word is *kevala,* which, because of the *sandhi*, could be either nominative (*kevalaḥ)* or locative (*kevale*). *Kevala* means "only" or even "the absolute," so here the locative case has been translated as "in the absolute."

[15] The word here is *ātmā-saṃstha*, "situated in the *ātmā.*" So depending on the interpretation of *ātmā,* there is a wide range of meaning. Here I have taken *ātmā* as body. Most translators take it as self or soul. Taking *ātmā* as self or soul is too abstract and unnecessary in this case.

[16] That is to say, the *jīvātmā* and the *paramātmā.*

[17] There are two forms of light, heavenly light, in the form of the sun, and earthly light, in the form of fire. Both symbolize the light of knowledge.

manifest within the body.

14. Taking one's body as the lower wood and the syllable *om* as the fire drill, and by rubbing the two in meditation, as it were, these hidden gods, the soul and the super-soul, can be perceived within the body.

15-16. As sesame oil can be found within sesame seeds, as butter can be found in milk, as water can be found within a dried riverbed, or as fire can be found in wood, so the soul can be found within the body through meditation and austerity. In this way, that all-pervading spiritual essence[16] that exists within the body can be found like butter in milk. This is the knowledge of *brahma* rooted in austerity and introspection taught in these teachings. Indeed, this is the teaching!

Here ends the First *Adhyāya*

Second *Adhyāya*

1. May the sun inspire our mind and thoughts as we begin this search for truth. Recognizing fire as light, Savitri brought light to this world in the form of fire.[17]

2. With our minds focused, we worship that divine sun for power and the attainment of heaven.

3. With our minds controlled and our thoughts focused on that divine realm, may the sun inspire our senses to perceive that mighty and radiant reality.

4. The wise fix their mind and thoughts on that great all-knowing *brahma* and offer oblations and prayers to that divine sun who is praised on high.

5. With respect I join those ancient prayers. May my prayers follow the path of light. May the offspring of the immortals, who reside in divine abodes, hear my prayers.

6. Where fire is kindled, where the wind blows, where soma overflows, there the perfect yogic mind arises.[18]

7. With the blessing of Savitri, the sun, practice these ancient teachings and make them your shelter. Thus you will be released from sin.

8. Holding the body steady, with the chest, neck and head in line, the *yogī* should draw the senses and the mind into the heart. In this way he can cross the river of sorrow using the boat of knowledge.

---

[18] This verse alludes to the practice of meditational yoga. "Fire" means the serpent power of *kuṇḍalinī*. Yogic meditation kindles this fire. Wind is the breath controlled during *prāṇayama*. Breath is the wind of the body. *Soma* is the elixir mentioned throughout the Vedas. It is also the mind controlled through breath control and meditation. "The mind arises" means the perfect yogic mind arises.

[19] While practicing meditation, the *yogī* successively "sees," in his yogic vision, the following impressions as his meditation deepens: mist, wind, sun, etc. These are impressions that the *yogī* feels within his body and mind during meditation.

9. Let the *yogī* practice breath control to restrain his bodily functions by diminishing the breath. And like a chariot yoked with untrained horses, let him firmly control the mind.

10. Let the *yogī* follow this practice in a place that is level and clean, free of rocks, gravel and fire. It should be a place that is quiet and pleasing to the mind and the eye, and that is in a secluded place protected from the wind.

11. As the *yogī* advances in practice he will experience mist, smoke, sun, wind, fire, fireflies, lightning, crystal, and finally the moon as he draws closer to *brahma*.[19]

12. During the practice of yoga the body of the *yogī*, which is made of the five essential elements, earth, water, fire, air and space, along with their objects, begins to change, and by the fire of this yoga the *yogī* eventually becomes free of the sufferings of disease and old age.

13. As the process of yoga proceeds, lightness of the body, good health, freedom from longing, a bright complexion, pleasantness of voice, a sweet odor, and decreased excretions all arise.

14. As a mirror smeared in clay shines after it has been cleaned, so the embodied soul in this world shines and becomes free of all sorrows upon realizing the nature of soul.

15. By understanding the nature of the individual soul, which shines like a lamp, one can know the nature of *brahma*. By

knowing the nature of *brahma,* who is unborn, eternal and free of all hint of matter, one becomes free from the knots of this world.[20]

16. This divine shining One exists in all places. He appears within the heart of the firstborn in this world; he appears alongside the child in the womb. He has appeared in the past and will appear in the future. With faces everywhere, He stands behind all beings as their foundation.

17. To this God, who exists within fire and water, who has entered within all beings, who is within the trees and herbs, to that God I offer homage. Indeed, I bow to that Divine Being.

Here Ends the Second *Adhyāya*

---

[20] This could be restated: By knowing the nature of the *jīvātmā,* one can know the nature of the *paramātmā;* and when one knows these two, one knows *brahma.*

[21] The word is *rudra,* and it literally means "terrible." Here in verses 2-6, it refers to Rudra, who in later Hinduism is Shiva. In this chapter of the Upanishad we see the seed of a later idea, that God exists in three forms: as a person, *bhagavan;* as an indwelling spirit, *paramātmā;* and an abstract force, *brahma.* As we see reference to God as Rudra, the Terrible, this is God as a person, *bhagavan.* Verses 8-9 talk about God as *puruṣa,* which I take to be the later idea of *paramātmā,* indwelling spirit. Finally, verse 10 refers to the abstract idea of God as beyond all form and categorization. This is *brahma.* See the Bhagavat Purana 1.2.11

[22] The verbal form is *dhamati,* from *dhmā,* meaning to blow. The reference is to a blacksmith, who forges metal by blowing the fire.

Third Adhyāya

1. This Divine One casts the net of illusion and rules as a sovereign over all these worlds. He oversees the rise and maintenance of beings. Those who understand this attain immortality.

2. He is Rudra, the Terrible.[21] The knowers of *brahma* understand Him as one without a second. By His sovereign power He rules these worlds. As the ruler of these worlds, He stands over all beings as their source and destruction.

3. With eyes in all places and faces on all sides, with arms and feet in all directions, this divine One fashions[22] heaven and earth with his arms and wings.[23]

4. This Terrible One, the great seer and the ruler of all, who is the source and origin of the gods, in the beginning created the seed of the universe.[24] May He endow us with clear intellect.

5. O Rudra, your auspicious form is without terror or faults. As you dwell in the most secret places, kindly look down upon us and bless us with your auspicious form.

---

[23] Here the reference is to an ironsmith, who uses his arms to beat metal into shape. The reference to wings refers to a blacksmith who fans the fire to create more heat to work metal.

[24] The Sanskrit word is *hiraṇya-garbha*, which is literally "golden egg."

6. O Dweller on High, the arrow you hold in your hand ready to throw, make that arrow auspicious. Harm no man or beast.

7. Higher than this[25] is the Supreme, the highest *brahma,* who dwells hidden in the body of every being. By knowing this Lord, who pervades this entire universe, one becomes immortal.

8. I know this immense *puruṣa*[26] who is beyond darkness and who is radiant like the sun. Knowing Him one surpasses death. There is no other way to reach this goal.

9. This whole world is pervaded by this *puruṣa*. Nothing surpasses this *puruṣa*, nothing is smaller or greater than this *puruṣa*. Like a great tree He stands fixed in all His glory.[27]

---

[25] There is some question as to what is meant by "higher than this," *tataḥ param.* Does it mean higher than Rudra, or higher than material nature or something else?

[26] Literally, the word means "man." Here the idea is more like "cosmic man" and suggests the idea of indwelling spirit, generic personality, if you will. This is the idea of *paramātmā.*

[27] This could also be read as "stands fixed in heaven."

[28] This is the idea of God beyond all form, *brahma.*

[29] Here the word is *śiva,* and the question arises whether this is a specific reference to the God Shiva or the word in its generic sense, "auspicious" or "beautiful." Translators, of course, will take it one way or another according to their theological perspective.

[30] The word is *prāpti,* which is a "gift" or "prize." Many commentators say the prize is *mukti*, liberation.

10. Yet still higher is that God who is formless and beyond all conceptions.[28] Those who understand this become immortal; others continue to suffer in this world.

11. This all-pervading Lord with faces, heads and necks in all places, who dwells in the heart of all beings, is the omnipresent Lord.[29]

12. This great Lord, the *puruṣa*, is the author of existence. He is an inextinguishable light who rules over this great and wonderful gift.[30]

13. This *puruṣa,* the size of a thumb, is the inner soul. He dwells in the heart of beings. He has to be contemplated with heart, intellect and mind. Those who know this become immortal.

14. This *puruṣa*[31] exists with a thousand heads, a thousand eyes, and a thousand feet. This Being covers the earth on all sides and

---

[31] The word used here is *puruṣa,* which literally means "man." There are actually three *puruṣas* mentioned in this hymn, this first one and two more mentioned in verse 5. This first *puruṣa* could be called the *mahā-puruṣa,* or "main *puruṣa.*" Here it has been translated as "cosmic being." The second *puruṣa* is mentioned in verse 5 as *virāj,* the splendorous one, who has evolved from the first *puruṣa* mentioned here. From the *virāj puruṣa* comes a third *puruṣa,* who is also referenced in verse 5. It is this third *puruṣa* who is the object of sacrifice mentioned from verse 5 on.

even extends beyond in all directions.[32]

15. This *puruṣa* is the universe, including everything that has been and everything that will be. He is the Lord of the immortals[33] and of all those who grow by food.[34]

16. With hands and feet in all places, with eyes, heads, faces and ears on all sides, this Lord envelops all.

17. Appearing to possess the power of all the senses, this Lord

---

[32] The word used here is *daśāṅgula*, "ten fingers." These ten fingers are the ten directions, the eight usual directions plus up and down.

[33] Literally, the Lord of immortality, *amṛtatvasya iśānaḥ*

[34] Literally, "through food he grows beyond."

[35] The city of nine gates is the body.

[36] Here the individual soul is referred to as a swan (*haṃsa*). The implication is that the cosmic man, the *puruṣa,* enters a body as an individual soul and so moves about in this external world.

[37] The word used here is *lelāyate,* which comes from the verb *lī,* to "quiver" or "shake." *Lī* also makes the word *līlā,* which is "play." The idea is that this Lord enters this world as the individual soul and so moves about "playing" in this physical world.

[38] The word is *bahis,* Literally, it means "outside."

[39] This soul is called Lord because he is free to go anywhere in this physical world and inhabit any form of life. "Moving" means all species that can move about; "non moving" means such species as trees and plants, which do not have freedom of movement.

[40] The word is *deva* and could also be translated as "shining one."

[41] The word is *avarṇa*, which is literally "without color."

is without senses. He is the controller of all and the great shelter of the world.

18. In the city of nine gates[35] the embodied swan[36] moves about[37] in this physical world.[38] He is the Lord of all the worlds, including both the moving and nonmoving worlds.[39]

19. Without feet he moves swiftly; without hands he seizes all things. Without eyes he sees all; and without ears he hears all. He knows all things and yet no one knows him. He is therefore called the great primal Person.

20. Smaller than the smallest, larger than the largest, this *ātmā* is hidden in the heart of beings. When, by the grace of the creator, a person is able to perceive this Lord who sits without activity in the hearts of beings, he becomes free of all sorrow.

21. I know this ancient and imperishable One who is the Soul of all and who is present in all places due to His all-pervasiveness. Those knowers of *brahma* always proclaim him as the one who brings about the cessation of birth.

Here ends the Third *Adhyāya*

Fourth *Adhyāya*

1. May that God,[40] who is without material qualities,[41] who creates qualities in this world according to a hidden purpose, who in the beginning sends forth this universe and who, in the

end, winds it back, may He endow us with clear intellect.

2. He is the sun and the moon. He is fire and water. He is the wind and the stars. He is the Lord of creatures and He is *brahma.*

3. Your face is everywhere: You are a woman. You are a man. You are a youth. You are a maiden. You are an old man hobbling about with a staff.

4. You are a dark blue bee. You are a green bird with red eyes. You are the rain cloud filled with lightning. You are the seasons

---

[42] The billy goat is the individual soul and the nanny goat is material nature. Red, white and black may refers to the past, present and future, or fire, water and earth, or even the three *guṇas* of Sankhya philosophy: *rajas*, *sattva* and *tamas*. The other billy goat, who moves away, is the soul in this world who seeks liberation. That soul is finished trying to enjoy in this world.

[43] This verse can also be found in RV 1.164.20 and then again in Mundaka 3.1.1. The two birds are the two *puruṣa*, the *jīvātmā* and the *paramātmā.*

[44] Both the individual soul (*jīvātmā*) and the supreme soul (*paramātmā*) are called *puruṣas.* Here the reference is to the individual soul.

[45] Literally, the controller of *māyā.* The word *māyā,* in its most basic form, simply means a trick or an illusion of magic. In the later *vedānta* of Shankara, it came to mean illusion in the sense that this whole world is unreal, an illusion. This is not the meaning intended here.

[46] The other is the individual soul, *jīvātmā,* who eats the fruits of this world and so suffers.

and the seas. You are without beginning. You are all-pervading. You are the source of all these worlds.

5. A billy goat lies down with a nanny goat. She is red, white and black. They enjoy and many offspring are born. Another billy goat, who has already enjoyed, rejects her and moves away.[42]

6. Two birds, who are companions, live on the same tree. One tastes the fruit of the tree while the other simply looks on.[43]

7. Both are on the same tree. One *puruṣa,*[44] the living being, is entangled and suffers due to his powerlessness. But seeing the other *puruṣa,* the Supreme, who is happy and majestic in his Lordship, his suffering vanishes.

8. The Vedas point to a higher realm beyond this physical world wherein the immortals dwell. But what is the use of the Vedas for one who does not understand this? Yet for those who do understand, they come to know *brahma.*

9. The Magician[45] creates this world along with the meters, the sacrifices, the rites and religious observances. He creates the past and the future, and all that the Vedas proclaim. The others,[46] however, are controlled by this magic.

10. That Great Lord is the magician and material nature is the illusion. This whole world is pervaded by the things that come from Him.

11. That God presides over all species of life.[47] From Him this world springs forth and from Him it is wound up. He is praised as the Lord who bestows all gifts, and those who understand Him attain unparalleled peace.

12. That Rudra, who is the great seer and Lord of all, who is the source of all the gods, who witnessed the birth of the creator,[48] may He grant us pure intelligence.

13. To that One, who is the God of the gods, in whom the worlds take shelter, who is the Lord of both two-footed and four-footed creatures, let us make sacrificial offerings to Him.

14. Knowing the One who is finer than the finest, with many forms, as the One who creates the universe out of chaos, this beautiful One who alone encompasses all the worlds, one who knows Him in this way attains unparalleled peace.

15. He is the protector and maintainer of this temporal world.

---

[47] The expression is *yoniṃ yonim,* meaning each and every womb. A womb is an access point into this world.

[48] *Hiraṇya-garbha*, the golden egg generally refers to the creator God Brahmā, who is born from a golden egg.

[49] "When there is no darkness," which is to say when there is no duality. When there is no up, there is no down.

[50] The exact word is *śiva*. Here it has been glossed as *brahma*. It could refer to the specific god Shiva or to meaning of the word itself as auspicious or propitious.

[51] This is the first *pada* of the *gāyatrī* mantra found in RV 3.62.10.

[52] Literally, "show me the right side of your face."

He is the Lord of all the worlds even though he is hidden from all beings. He is the one the gods and the divine sages cherish. Those who know this sever the fetters of mortality.

16. He is exceedingly fine, like the sheen on oil. He is the hidden beauty in all beings. He alone is the God who pervades all these worlds. One who knows this becomes freed from all entanglements.

17. This God is the maker of all things. He is the Great Soul, who is seated in the heart of all creatures. He can be contemplated with heart, insight and mind. Those who know this become immortal.

18. When there is no darkness,[49] there is no day or night, no being or nonbeing. *Brahma*[50] alone exists. That immutable *brahma* is the meaning of the "that" in the verse "*tat-savitur vareṇyam.*"[51] From "that" this ancient wisdom has come forth.

19. Not from above, not from the middle and not from below can this *brahma* be understood. Nothing compares to Him. He is therefore All Famous.

20. No one can see His form. He cannot be seen with the eye. But those who do perceive Him do so with the heart and mind. They see Him situated within the heart and so become immortal.

21-22. "O Lord, you are unborn! O Terrible One, look at me.[52] Give me all protection. Do not harm my children, do not harm my descendants. Give me longevity. Do not harm my cattle or my horses. Slay not our heroes in anger. With offerings in hand we call on you." Those in awe and fear approach Him in this way.

Here ends the Fourth *Adhyāya*

Fifth *Adhyāya*

1. In the eternal and indestructible city of *brahma* two things are hidden, *vidyā* and *avidyā. Vidyā* leads to the immortal and *avidyā* leads to the perishable. Yet *brahma*, who rules this city, is beyond both *vidyā* and *avidyā*.

2. *Brahma* rules all species and other forms of life. In the beginning it was He who witnessed the birth of the seer Kapila[53] and nurtured him with this knowledge.

---

[53] This is an obscure reference. Kapila is the founder of the Sankhya system of philosophy, but it is not clear that the word *kapila* refers to this Kapila. Instead commentators suggest the reference is to *hiraṇya-garbha*, the creator God Brahmā, who is born from a golden egg.

[54] The Upanishads.

[55] This reference is obscure, but the verse may refer to the path leading to the gods (*devayāna*), the path leading to the ancestors (*pitriyāna*) or the path that only leads to rebirth.

[56] The three qualities are the three *guṇa*, goodness, passion and darkness, *sattva*, *rajas* and *tamas*.

[57] *Ahaṅkāra*, literally "I am the doer."

3. This God casts a net into this world and pulls it together. Having created this world, He then dissolves it. In this way He is the great Soul and Lord of all.

4. As the sun shines and illumines all regions, above, below and beyond, so this God, the highest Lord, rules all those who take birth in this world.

5. He is the creator of the universe and the one who enables all things to function according to their nature. He brings maturity to all things and stands over these worlds. He creates diversity in all things.

6. O learned ones, these teachings are hidden in the mystical teachings[54] of the Vedas. They reveal *brahma*. The gods and sages of the past understood this and so absorbed themselves in *brahma* and thereby became immortal.

7. The individual soul wanders throughout this world on three paths[55] according to his own actions and so assumes various forms. Being controlled by the three qualities,[56] he initiates action and its result and so enjoys and suffers all that he has done.

8. In fact the individual soul is luminous like the sun and is endowed with volition and a sense of self.[57] He is situated within the heart and has the measure of one thumb's length. But bound by the qualities of matter while residing in a body, the soul appears no bigger than a mere dot and is without power.

9. Take the tip of a hair and split it into a hundred parts and then split one of those parts into a hundred parts. This is the conceived size of the soul. And even though it is tiny, it is infinite.

10. This soul is not male, nor even neuter. Whatever body it accepts, it identifies with that body.

11. By the enchantment arising from imagination, touch and sight,[58] and by the nourishment of food and drink, a body is born and grows. In this way the embodied soul continually assumes various forms in various places according to its actions performed.

12. The embodied soul assumes endless forms, both gross and subtle, according to its desires.[59] By virtue of its actions and mental state,[60] the embodied soul creates its position in the

---

[58] The reference here is sexual.

[59] The word is *guṇa,* which I have glossed as desire. Literally it means qualities.

[60] The word is *ātmā,* and apart from the regular "soul" and "self" meanings, it can have the meaning of "body" or, in this case, "mind."

[61] The word used here is *svabhava,* which is literally "inherent nature." Some view the inherent nature of matter as the cause of creation.

[62] The expression is *brahma-cakra*, the wheel of *brahma.* So the verse may be rendered "It is the greatness of God which keeps the *brahman*-wheel turning."

[63] "The one" is generally understood to be *puruṣa;* the two *vyakta* and *avyakta*, the manifest and unmanifest; "the three" the three *guṇas: sattva*, *rajas* and *tamas*, goodness, passion and darkness; and, finally, "the eight" the constituents of matter: earth, water, fire, air, space, mind, intellect and identity. See BG 7.4

world even though in fact it is different from the things it becomes.

13. When one knows that shining One who assumes unlimited forms and is the creator of the universe in the midst of disorder, who is without beginning or end and who envelops the universe, one becomes freed from all bonds.

14. Those who know this divine One who is the creator of both the whole and its parts, who is all-auspicious and who is the creator of existence and even of nonexistence, who has no physical body and yet can be conceived in the heart, soon cast off their bodies.

Here ends the Fifth *Adhyāya*

Sixth *Adhyāya*

1. Some say that matter itself is the cause of creation,[61] others say it is time, but both are wrong. In fact, it is the greatness of God which alone keeps this world in motion.[62]

2. From the beginning this God has enveloped the entire universe. He is the knower, the architect of time, and is complete with all qualities and omniscience. By His sanction alone does this world made of earth, water, fire, air and space exist. This must be understood!

3-4. Repeatedly this God creates and then winds up this creation. When He creates He brings together the essence of all things, including the one, the two, the three, and the eight,[63] along with time and the subtle and diverse qualities of matter.[64] The activities of creation are full of these qualities and it is He who apportions all states. And when creation is wound up, all that has been done is destroyed and comes to an end. He alone remains.

5. This God is primeval. He is the cause and basis of creation. He is beyond past, present, and future. He is unified without parts. This Lord, who exists in the heart and who assumes unlimited forms, should be worshipped as the source of existence.

6. On this tree of life He is beyond form and time, yet this manifest world arises from Him. He is the source of *dharma* and the destroyer of evil. He is the Lord of opulence. He is the ultimate abode and the giver of immortality, who is situated in the heart of all beings.

7. Let us find this highest Lord amongst lords, the greatest divinity amongst all divinities, the master among masters, the

---

[64] This Upanishad appears to be referring to later Sankaya philosophy.

[65] There is a qualifying word that has not been translated here: *niṣkriya*. It means without moving. It is an obscure reference, but in essence says that the many souls of this world are inactive. Commentators have difficulties explaining why the unlimited souls of this world are inactive.

[66] See KathU 5.13. The first two lines are identical. The words are *nitya* and *cetana*. *Nitya* means eternal and *cetana* means sentient, so both the *jīvātmā* and the *paramātmā* are called *nitya* and *cetana.* But the prime *nitya* and the prime *cetana* are the *paramātmā*.

highest of the high, the adorable Lord of this universe.

8. He has no physical body or senses, yet no one equals or surpasses Him. His powers are diverse indeed. All His actions, strength and knowledge are innate.

9. No one is His lord or master. He is invisible. He is the creator and the master of the senses. He has no father or sovereign.

10. As a spider spins a web and hides itself within, so that God creates this world and hides Himself within. May that God grant us entrance into *brahma.*

11. This One God, hidden in all beings, pervades this entire universe. He is the inner soul of all, the overseer of action who dwells in all elements. He is the solitary witness and the animator devoid of material qualities.

12. He is the sole Lord of the many.[65] He plants one seed that becomes many. Those steadfast souls know Him as situated in the heart. They alone find eternal happiness.

13. The One constant among all constants, the One conscious among the conscious many,[66] He is the One among the many who grants all wishes. Through the practice of yoga and *sānkhya,* those who know Him as the ultimate cause are freed from all fetters in this world.

14. In His realm the sun does not shine, nor even the stars, the

moon, lightning or even fire. He alone shines, and through his light all else shines.[67]

15. He is the swan[68] in this world. He is the fire which has entered water.[69] Knowing Him one passes beyond death. There is no other way.

16. He is the creator and the knower of all things, the source, the architect of time, the possessor of qualities and the reservoir of knowledge. He alone is the cause of the *pradhāna,*[70] and along with the individual souls, He is the ruler of qualities and the One who grants liberation or bondage in this world of rebirth.

---

67 See BG 15.6. KathU 5.15, MundU 2.2.10.

68 The word is *haṃsa*, which is actually a kind of goose. "Swan" makes a more poetic translation. This "swan" is a symbol for the *jīvātmā* or the *paramātmā.*

69 Here water means the body, which is basically made of water, and fire is the *paramātmā*. So the swan in the form of *paramātmā* dwells in the body along with the *jīvātmā.*

70 In Sāṅkhya philosophy *pradhāna* is primordial matter and the source of *prakṛti.*

71 This analogy seems odd. Perhaps the meaning is a fire that is smokeless, as when wood is reduced to just coals.

72 In other words, it will never happen.

73 The word is *vedānta,* which here has been generalized as "Vedic teaching," but in later Hinduism became identified with specific systems of theology, i.e., Advaita, Vashishtha and, Dvaita Vedanta.

17. This One who is made of One substance, who is immortal, and who exists as the controller, the knower, the all-pervading One and the protector of the Universe, rules this world eternally. There is no other cause beyond this Lord.

18. He is the One who in ancient times created Brahmā, the first-born, and entrusted him with the Vedas. Desiring liberation I take shelter of this God who shines with His own intellect.

19. He is without parts, unmoving, tranquil, unblemished, and blameless. Indeed, He is the highest bridge to immortality. He is like a fire whose fuel is spent.[71]

20. Only when men are able to roll up the sky like a piece of leather will it be possible to put an end to suffering without first knowing God.[72]

21. By the power of austerities and the grace of God, the learned Shvetashvatara achieved *brahma* and then proclaimed these teachings to the highest sages as the supreme means of purification and for the delight of the community of ascetics.

22. This supreme secret of Vedic knowledge[73] was first declared in a former age. It must not be spoken to one who is not tranquil or who is not a son or a disciple.

23. This subject matter, which has been declared in these teachings, shines in one who has deep devotion to both God and teacher. Indeed, this knowledge shines forth in such a person.

Here ends the sixth *Adhyāya*

Here ends the Shvetashvatara Upanishad

8

Mundaka Upanishad

Introduction to

Mundaka Upanishad

The Mundaka Upanishad is ascribed to the Atharva Veda. The word *muṇḍaka* has been the subject of discussion. It literally means "shaven" or "barber." Given this title, some have suggested that this Upanishad was composed for shaven-headed ascetics, *yatis*. They have interpreted the "head-vow" (*sirovrata*) mentioned at the conclusion of the Upanishad as a reference to the shaving of the head and as another indication that the text was meant for ascetics. Although such an interpretation is plausible, especially in light of the Mundaka's anti-ritual attitude and its use of the terms *yati* (MuU 3.1.5; 3.2.6) and *sannyasa* (MuU 3.2.6), I do not think it is certain. The text also uses the term *muṇḍaka* for "chapter."

More than any other Upanishad, the Mundaka Upanishad challenges both Vedic ritualism and the Vedic texts that embody the ritual tradition. It establishes a clear distinction between a lower class of religious knowledge, the old Vedic texts and ancillary literature, and a higher class of knowledge consisting of texts that teach the imperishable *brahma* obtained through direct realization in the form of meditation. It is this higher knowledge that the Mundaka Upanishad refers to as *vedānta* (3.2.6), one of the earliest recorded uses of this significant term.

First *Mundaka*
First *Khaṇḍa*

1. Brahmā[1] is firstborn among the gods. He is the creator and the guardian of the universe. To his oldest son, Atharvan, he taught *brahma-vidyā,*[2] the foundation of all knowledge.

2. Atharvan then spoke this ancient knowledge to Angir, who in turn spoke it to Bharadvaja Satyavaha, who then spoke it to Angiras,[3] in both its higher and lower forms.[4]

---

[1] The stem of this word is *brahman* and it comes in two genders, masculine and neuter. As a masculine noun it declines as *brahmā* in its first case ending. As a neuter noun, it declines as *brahma* (no long *ā* at the end). Brahmā as a masculine noun is the creator god. *Brahma* as a neuter noun is the imperishable force or substratum that pervades all life. Here the gender is clearly masculine, and so it refers to the creator god, Brahmā, who is the first-created of all the gods.

[2] *Brahma-vidyā* is literally "knowledge of *brahma.*" From a certain perspective, all knowledge is *brahma*-knowledge since everything comes from *brahma.*

[3] This is a *parampara*, a discipular succession.

[4] Knowledge of *brahma* comes in two forms, higher and lower knowledge. In the Isha Upanishad, and in other places, these two kinds of knowledge are mentioned as *vidyā* and *avidyā*. Here it is called lower and higher knowledge (*parāvara*). We understand higher knowledge as spiritual knowledge and lower knowledge as secular knowledge or perhaps practical knowledge. Both are important.

3. Shaunaka,[5] a wealthy householder, then approached Angiras in the proper manner[6] and inquired, "Reverend sir, what is it that should be known that explains all this?"[7]

4. Angiras replied: Knowers of *brahma* say that knowledge has two forms, higher knowledge and lower knowledge. Both must be known.

5. Higher knowledge is that learning which brings one closer to the Imperishable.[8] Lower knowledge is that learning found in

---

[5] Shaunaka is a wealthy landowner who is mentioned in the Puranas. Here he is mentioned as being a disciple of Angiras.

[6] "In the proper manner" refers to the process whereby a student approaches a teacher and becomes a disciple.

[7] "All this" means "this universe" or "this world." The question being asked here is effectively the perennial question, What is the meaning of life?

[8] The word here is *akṣara*, the imperishable.

[9] In this later Upanishad we begin to see a rejection of the four Vedas as a source of ultimate knowledge. In even later works like the BG, there are many references to the "flowery words of the Vedas" (2.42) and how the Vedas are a distraction to the attainment of *mokṣa* and *bhakti*. Such a rejection or lessening of Vedic authority is unheard of and even blasphemy in the early Upanishads. Phonetics, ritual, grammar, etymology, meter, and astronomy are the six *vedāngas* or six supplements that support Vedic learning.

[10] The word used here is *tapasā*, "through heat."

[11] Here the *brahma* being referred to is this physical world. It is a world characterized by name, form and variegation. We might call the world we see all around us the manifest *brahma*.

the Rig, Yajur, Sama and Atharva Vedas, including phonetics, ritual, grammar, etymology, meter, and astronomy.[9]

6. What the wise see as the source of all things is imperceptible, ungraspable, and without family or caste. It cannot be seen or heard. It is without hands or feet, and it is eternal, omnipresent, all-pervading. It is fine beyond measure.

7. As a spider sends out a web and then draws it back, as vegetation grows from the earth, as hair grows from the body, so all beings grow from this Imperishable One.

8. Through heat[10] the power of *brahma* expands and food is created. From food, breath, mind, the elements, all these worlds along with action, and even immortality, arise.

9. From this all-knowing One, whose power consists of the wisdom derived from full knowledge, arises this *brahma* that we see before us full of name, form and food.[11]

Here ends the First *Khaṇḍa*

Second *Khaṇḍa*

Here is a truth:

1. Those rites which have been divined by the learned seers in the Vedic mantras are spread throughout the three Vedas. Perform them always and with faith, O lovers of truth. They are

your path to the world of those who practice these rites in the proper way.

2. After the fire has been kindled and the flame is stable, add your oblations between the two portions of ghee that have been offered into the fire.

3. That fire sacrifice, however, which is performed without the new moon or full moon sacrifices, or the four months or the harvest moon sacrifices, which is without guests or the oblations to all the gods, or that neglects the rules, will destroy the performer's worlds all the way up to the seventh.[12]

---

[12] It is not clear what is meant by the seventh. One possibility is the earth and the six planes above it. Another is seven family generations.

[13] Respectively: black, terrific, swift as thought, very red, bright smoke, scintillating, all-glowing.

[14] The number eighteen is obscure. One interpretation is sixteen priests, plus the sacrificer and his wife. Another is the four Vedas together with the Samhitas, the Brāhmanas, the Sūtras and the six Vedāngas.

[15] The word here is *iṣṭāpūrta* and it means "one's stock of merit." This refers to the accumulation of merit (*punya*) that comes from the performance of pious rites and good works such as feeding the poor, digging wells, and other good works, that promote community welfare. As one builds up one's "reservoir" of good deeds, one can be born in a better situation, even in higher worlds where life improves dramatically. As one enjoys this stock of good deeds, it becomes consumed, after which the person descends back to his starting position. One falls from heaven, so to speak. It's like going on a vacation: Once one's time and money have been exhausted, one must return home.

4. Fire has seven flickering tongues: *kālī, karālī, manojavā, sulohitā, sudhūmra-varṇa, sphuliṅganī, and viśvarucī.*[13]

5. One should perform these rites and make offerings at the proper time when these tongues are strong and bright. As the sun's rays, these tongues will carry the performer to where the One God, who is the Lord of all gods, dwells.

6. Honoring and praising this performer of sacrifice, these blazing tongues call out, "Come, come! Let us carry you by the rays of the sun to the realm of Brahmā, which is built on great merit and good deeds."

7. Indeed, these eighteen[14] are unanchored boats. They are inferior rites; yet the fools who praise them as the best return once again to old age and death.

8. These fools, thinking of themselves as learned, wallow in ignorance and so harm themselves as the blind are led by the blind.

9. Wallowing in ignorance and acting like children, they think we have accomplished our purpose! Out of passion these fools, who are attached to rituals, do not understand. Wretched, they fall from heaven when their merit is exhausted.

10. Thinking that building up merit[15] is the highest goal, these fools know nothing better. Having exhausted their merit, which kept them on top of heaven, they fall down and enter inferior worlds.

11. But those who dwell in the forest, practicing austerities with faith, who are learned, peaceful and living on alms, are free of passion. Passing through the gate of the sun, they seek that immortal Person who is all-pervading.

12. A *brāhmaṇa* must examine these worlds that are built on works and rites and should become indifferent to them. The eter-

---

[16] The Sanskrit reads, *nāsty akṛta kṛtena*, "There is no unmade through the made." The made worlds are these worlds we see before us, that are the results of a cause. The unmade worlds comprise the realm of *brahma* that has no natural cause. The worlds one obtains through rites are *kṛta,* made, while the immortal realm of *brahma* is *akṛta,* unmade. Therefore, the performance of the good works that sustain this world has no bearing on the eternal realm of *brahma.*

[17] As a single spark has the same qualities as the fire from which it comes, so the individual soul has the same characteristics as *brahma,* from which it comes.

[18] There is a huge debate within Hindu theology as to whether God is ultimately an impersonal force or some kind of Supreme Person. In this chapter and in many other places throughout the Upanishads, the word *puruṣa* is used in conjunction with the word *akṣara. Puruṣa* literally means man, but it is also used to mean the soul and God. The word therefore implies a person, that the soul and God are persons. The word *akṣara* is an adjective that means "imperishable," and so it can apply to God as an imperishable person, *puruṣa*, or God as an imperishable force, *brahma*. In this verse the words are *puruṣa... akṣarāt paratah parah,* meaning that the *puruṣa* is beyond or higher than (*para*) the farthest imperishable. In this case, contextually *akṣara* is used as a description of *brahma.* This means that *puruṣa* is higher or beyond the *akṣara brahma*, which suggests God as a person is beyond God as force.

nal is not achieved by the non-eternal.[16] To understand this, let him go, wood in hand, to a teacher versed in knowledge and focused on *brahma*.

13. Let him approach, in the proper way, that learned teacher who can proclaim this knowledge of *brahma* by which the imperishable Person can be truly known to the student who is focused and peaceful.

Here ends the Second *Khaṇḍa*
Here ends the First *Muṇḍaka*

Second *Muṇḍaka*
First *Khaṇḍa*

Here is a truth:

1. O gentle one, as a thousand sparks burst forth from a blazing fire, all with the same form,[17] so diverse beings burst forth from the imperishable *brahma* only to return.

2. This Supreme Person (*Puruṣa*) is without form. He exists both within and outside of all things. He is unborn, without breath or mind, radiant and higher than even the imperishable *brahma*.[18]

3. From this One comes breath, mind, and all the senses, along with space, wind, light, water, and the earth, which supports all things.

4. Fire is His head. The sun and the moon are His eyes. The directions are His ears. His speech proclaims the Vedas. The wind is His breath. The universe is His heart and the earth is His feet. He is the inner soul of all beings.

5. From this *Puruṣa* comes fire, which is the fuel of the sun. Rains come from the moon, by which all vegetation flourishes on earth. A male pours his seed[19] into a female and thereby creatures are born.

6. From this *Puruṣa* the Rig, Sama, and Yajur Vedas arise, along with initiation, sacrifice, and all other rites, including sacrificial gifts. The year, the sacrificer, and all the worlds where the sun and the moon shine, all spring from this *Puruṣa.*

7. From this *Puruṣa* the many gods, celestials, men, animals and birds are born. The incoming and outgoing breaths, along with rice and barley, austerities, faith, truth, chastity, and the law, all arise from Him.

---

[19] There is a notion behind this that from grain comes the soul. Souls who have departed this world return through falling to earth in rain, which enters the earth and which ultimately gets transmitted into a man through the consumption of grains and then into semen and finally into the embryo.

[20] The word used here is *prāṇa,* which commonly means "breath." However, some commentators suggest it means the seven senses found in the head: the two eyes, two ears, two nostrils and the mouth.

[21] Here this expression is *guhāśaya,* "hidden in the secret place," meaning the innermost core of the body, i.e., the heart.

8. The seven breaths,[20] the seven flames, the seven kinds of fuel, the seven sacrifices, and the seven worlds all arise from this *Puruṣa*. This set of seven lays hidden within the cave of the heart and functions within every being.[21]

9. From this *Puruṣa* come the oceans and mountains. From Him flow the different rivers. From Him vegetation arises, along with the juice by which He dwells within all beings as their innermost soul.

10. Indeed, my friend, this *Puruṣa* is all things: action, austerities, and the immortal *brahma*. The one who knows this *Puruṣa* situated in the heart of the body is able to cut the knot of ignorance while living in this world.

Here ends the Second *Muṇḍaka*
Here ends the First *Khaṇḍa*

Second *Khaṇḍa*
First *Muṇḍaka*

1. There is a special place, openly manifest yet hidden, in the secret place. All that moves, breathes and blinks, all that is gross and subtle, dwells within this special place. It is most desirable yet beyond the understanding of beings.

2. Even though blazing, it is more subtle than the subtlest. All these worlds and all their inhabitants reside within. This is the imperishable *brahma*. It is breath. It is speech and mind. It is

truth and immortality. O noble one, seize it, seize it now!

3. These mystical teachings are a great weapon. Seize this bow and place an arrow sharpened with contemplation on this bow. Pull back that arrow and, with mind fully focused, strike this target, the imperishable *brahma.*

---

[22] The expression is *parāpara*, "higher and lower." Perhaps another translation could be "in all conditions," or even "in all species of life."

[23] The expression is *hiryan-maye pare kośe*, "in the highest *kośa* made of gold." A *kośa* is a container. Sometimes it is called a sheath. *Maya* here is a suffix that means "made of." In the TU (2.1-5) it is said that the soul is "wrapped" in five of these containers or sheaths: *anna-maya-kośa*, *prāna-maya-kośa*, *mano-maya-kośa*, *vijñāna-maya-kośa*, and the *ananda-maya-kośa*. The *anna-maya-kośa* is the container made of food (*anna*). This is the physical body. The *prāna-maya-kośa* is our "breath, or life-force (*prāna*) container." The *mano-maya-kośa* is our mental (*manas*) container. The *vijñāna-maya-kośa* is our intellectual container, sometimes called our wisdom body. Finally, the *ananda-maya-kośa* is our joy (*ananda*) container. So the questions arises, of these five containers, which one is the *hiryan-maya* container mentioned in this verse? In other words, which is the container that is "made of gold"? Commentators suggest it is the *vijñāna-kośa*, our intellect or wisdom body. In other language, this is our *buddhi*. As it has been noted, *brahma* is everywhere and encompasses all of these *kośas*, but the suggestion is that *brahma* can be more easily found through our intellect. This means that within meditation one should search the *vijñāna-maya-kośa* to most easily find the *ātmā* and thereby *brahma*.

4. The mystic syllable *om* is the bow. The *ātmā* is the arrow. *Brahma* is the target. With full attention, one must focus on that arrow and strike the target.

5. You must understand this *brahma* on which heaven, earth, sky, mind and breath are woven. Put aside other thoughts, for this is the bridge to immortality.

6. Like the spokes on a chariot that converge at the hub, the veins and arteries of the body converge at the heart. So the living beings move about within this network as they are constantly reborn. Reciting *om*, meditate on this *ātmā.* All blessings as you cross beyond darkness to the other shore!

7. Knowing and understanding all things, this *ātmā* dwells in glory on earth. Dwelling in the divine city of *brahma,* this *ātmā* is fixed in the heart. While dwelling in this body, which is made of food, he resides within the heart. He is the controller of breath and mind. In their wisdom, the wise can understand this and see that one's real form is immortal and shines with unbounded happiness.

8. When one sees this *ātmā* in all its forms, higher and lower,[22] the knot of attachment in the heart is cut, all doubts dissolve and the effects of karma melt away.

9. Those who know the *ātmā* understand that *brahma* exists pure and without division in the highest golden abode,[23] shining as the light of lights.

10. In that realm there is no need for sunlight, moonlight, or lightning, let alone fire.[24] There everything reflects the light of this One who shines in all glory.

11. This immortal *brahma* pervades this entire universe: north and south, east and west, above and below. Indeed, all this universe is *brahma*!

---

[24] See KathU 5.15 and ŚvetU 6.14 and BG 9.15

[25] This metaphor of the two birds first appears in the RV 1.164.20 then again in ShvetU 4.6.

[26] The word *puruṣa* primarily means man, but here and throughout the Upanishads it is used for both the cosmic man, i.e., God, as well as the individual soul, *ātmā*. So here two *puruṣas* dwell on the same tree of the body. One is the *paramātmā puruṣa* and the other is the *jīva-puruṣa*. The *jīva-puruṣa,* like a bird, hops from branch to branch, tasting all the fruits of this tree. In other words, the embodied individual soul experiences all the ups and downs of life. The other *puruṣa*, as *paramātmā,* just watches on. Eventually the individual soul becomes frustrated and turns to the *paramātmā puruṣa* for shelter. This is the beginning of yoga.

[27] Literally, the Sanskrit says "by the one who is not the Lord," *anīśayā*. This is likely a reference to *prakṛti*, material nature.

[28] The verse reads *puruṣaṃ brahma-yonim,* which could be rendered as "the Lord who is the source of *brahma"* or "the Lord whose source is *brahma* or "the Lord who is the source of Brahmā, the creator god."

[29] The text reads *satyam eva jayate nāṛtam*. The word *satyam* here is read as "the state of being *sat*," which is to say the "Real," but it could also be read as "truth." If it is rendered as truth, then, we can translate the verse as "Truth triumphs over non-truth. By truth the path to the gods opens wide. Learned seers whose desires have been fulfilled follow this path to the highest realm of truth."

Third *Muṇḍaka*
First *Khaṇḍa*

1. Two birds, companions and friends, nestle on the same fig tree. One eats the sweet fruit while the other just watches.[25]

2. On this tree one *puruṣa*[26] is sunk down and suffers, being deluded by material nature.[27] When this same *puruṣa* sees his companion and friend, the contented Lord in all His glory, his sorrows vanish.

3. When a learned seer perceives this Lord, who is the golden creator and source of *brahma,*[28] he shakes off the effects of both good and evil actions and becomes free of passion. He then attains the supreme state of this Lord.

4. *Ātmā,* in the form of life-force, shines through all living beings. Know this and proclaim it! Take pleasure in the *ātmā*! Rejoice in the *ātmā*! Act through the *ātmā.* Such a person is the best of those who know *brahma.*

5. This *ātmā* may be perceived through discipline and truth, proper knowledge and strict chastity, for the *ātmā* consists of light and exists within the heart. Ascetics whose faults have been cleansed can clearly see this radiant One,

6. Indeed, the Real prevails over the unreal.[29] Following the Real, the divine path opens wide. Learned seers whose desires

have been satisfied follow this path to that highest realm where the Real exists.

7. *Brahma* is great. *Brahma* is divine. Its form is inconceivable. It is finer than the finest. It is farther than the farthest and yet is close at hand. Hidden within the heart, it is here for those who strive to see it.

8. This *brahma* cannot be apprehended by the eye or any of the senses. It cannot be touched by words or attained through penance or acts of ritual sacrifice. It is through the blessings of knowledge that one's existence becomes purified and thereby this undifferentiated *brahma* can be seen in meditation.

9. Even while residing within the body with its five life-airs, this subtle *ātmā* can be known through meditation on the intellect.[30] This intellect pervades all beings through these life-airs,

---

[30] See fn 2.1.9 of this Upanishad.

[31] The word is *śukra,* which means semen. Crossing beyond semen means they are beyond rebirth.

[32] There is another way this verse can be read: "Only to the person whom the *ātmā* chooses does the *ātmā* choose to reveal its true form." This implies that it is only through the grace of the *ātmā* that the *ātmā* can be known, that no amount of personal endeavor can lead to realization of the *ātmā.* This is inconsistent with the tone of the Upanishads in general. Later, more devotional texts will invoke the need for divine grace. In this Upanishad and the Upanishads in general, realization of the *ātmā* can be obtained through a disciplined process of purification, learning and meditation.

and when it has been sharpened and purified, the *ātmā* shines through.

10. Whatever world the person with a disciplined and purified intellect desires, and whatever desires this person cherishes, he attains that world and those desires. Therefore, those who seek prosperity should honor this knower of the *ātmā*.

Here Ends the First *Khaṇḍa*

Second *Khaṇḍa*

1. This knower of the *ātmā* perceives the supreme realm of *brahma,* which shines brightly and is the foundation of this world. Those learned ones who are without desire and who worship the *puruṣa* cross beyond the seed of birth.[31]

2. A person who is full of desires and who mentally fixates on those desires is continually reborn throughout this world. But the one who has discovered the *ātmā* within himself becomes fulfilled, and so even while living in this world, his desires melt away.

3. This *ātmā* cannot be obtained through a teaching. This *ātmā* cannot be obtained through intellectualization. This *ātmā* cannot be obtained even through learning. Only to the person who desires and chooses the *ātmā* does this *ātmā* reveal its form.[32]

4. This *ātmā* cannot be realized by one who lacks determination,

nor by one who lacks focus, nor by one who undergoes penance without the mark.[33] But when a learned person strives by proper means he enters the realm of *brahma.*

5. Those sages who have entered this realm, whose understanding is mature, and who have perfected themselves and controlled their passions, find peace. Such determined and devoted souls enter the realm of the all-pervading *brahma.*[34]

6. Sages who have purified their existence through the yoga of

---

[33] The word is *aliṅga*, which is literally "without a mark." The reference is obscure. Some commentators suggest that *linga* means the marks of an ascetic or *sannyasi,* such as a shaven head, robes, etc. In other words, these teachings are only for a renunciate.

[34] The exact words are *sarvam eva āviśanti*, "they enter the All."

[35] The word used here is *sannyāsa.*

[36] The word used here is *vedānta*. Vedanta later became the name for a school of Hindu theology initially started by Shankara. Here the word is used in the general sense, to mean Vedic learning.

[37] In Hindu theology there is a school of learning known as Sankya, where the would is broken down into its constituent parts. Here, this is a *sāṅkya* type analysis of matter. In PU the fifteen parts are listed under 6.5.

[38] This is the *vijñāna-māyā kośa*. See fn MU 2.9 above.

[39] The exact words are *pare 'vyaye sarva ekī-bhavanti,* "They all become one in the supreme imperishable."

[40] The head vow, *śirovrata,* is likely shaving the head; in other words, becoming an ascetic. Some say this is a reference to a ritual described in the Atharva Veda that involves carrying fire on the head. The reference to the *ekarṣi* fire is obscure.

renunciation[35] and whose strict aim is the understanding of Vedic learning,[36] at the time of death are no longer reborn and so become immortal and enter the world of *brahma*.

7-8. When the fifteen parts[37] return to their source, when the senses return to their divinities, when the effects of action cease and the body made of intellect[38] merges into the Supreme;[39] as rivers flow to the ocean giving up their name and form, so the knower of the *ātmā,* being free of name and form, reaches the divine *puruṣa* in the highest abode.

9. The one who knows *brahma* becomes himself *brahma*. In his family no one is born who does not know *brahma.* Such a person overcomes all sorrows and sins. Being freed from the knot of the heart, he becomes immortal.

10. This doctrine has been described in the following verse: This knowledge of *brahma* must only be taught to those who have performed the necessary duties, who are versed in the Vedas and devoted to *brahma*. Such persons must have full faith and have offered themselves into the *ekarṣi* fire and performed the head vow according to the rule.[40]

11. This is the truth the seer Angiras taught in the past. One who has not performed the vows should not be taught this. Respects to the highest seer! Respects to the highest seer!

Here Ends the Second *Khaṇḍa*
Here Ends the Third *Muṇḍaka*
Here Ends the Mundaka Upanishad

9

Prashna Upanishad

Introduction to

Prashna Upanishad

The Prashna Upanisad is ascribed to the Atharva Veda. It consists of the sage Pippalada's answers to six questions posed by six learned Brahmins. The title of the Upanisad is derived from these questions as each of its six chapters is called a *praśna* or "question." Although the questions are diverse, they all focus on the importance of breath and salvation. And just like the earlier verse Upanisads, the Prashna Upanisad was composed, in all likelihood, as an independent text.

---

[1] Each of these sages come forward one at a time to ask a question. Each chapter of this Upanishad is therefore called a *praśna,* a question.

[2] "With wood in hand" means they approached the sage as students. In the *aśrama* or hermitage of the sage there would typically be a fire that needed to be tended. This would be the job of the sage's students.

[3] This may also be rendered "from where do beings come?"

[4] The word *rayi* means matter. The word *prāṇa* is breath. There is an intended sexual connotation, *rayi* is feminine while *prāṇa* is masculine. So as this couple comes together, beings are produced. The word *rayi* also means wealth; so as this couple comes together wealth is also created.

[5] Here the words are *mūrta* and *amūrta*. *Mūrta* means physical form. *Amūrta* would then be non physical form. I have glossed these two as gross and subtle form.

[6] In this world there is matter and spirit. This is the idea of these two words, *rayi* and *prāṇa.*

First *Praśna*

1. Sukesha Bharadvaja, Shaibya Satyakama, Sauryayani Gargya, Kaushalya Ashvalayana, Bhargava Vaidarbhi and Kabandhi Katyanana—all these men were intent on *brahma.*[1] Consequently, they searched for that highest *brahma,* and so, with wood in hand,[2] they approached the venerable Pippalada thinking, He can tell us everything.

2. The sage Pippalada spoke to them: "Remain here for a year. Practice austerities and chastity in full faith; then you may ask whatever you desire and, if I know, I will answer your questions."

3. After a year Kabandhi Katyanana approached the sage and asked, "Reverend Sir, from where does life come?"[3]

4. Pippalada replied, "Prajapati, the creator, naturally desires offspring, so he underwent austerities and produced a couple, *rayi* and *prāṇa,*[4] with the thought, 'These two will create creatures of all varieties.'

5. "The sun is *prāṇa* and the moon is *rayi*. In this world we see both gross and subtle[5] forms. All this is *rayi.*[6]

6-7. "As the sun rises, it enters the east and so bathes the world in its rays. Thereafter it moves to the other directions, including the nadir and the zenith, and so bathes all beings in its light. In this way the sun, as the universal fire, assumes numerous forms and illumines all life with its rays. In this regard there is the following verse:

8. "'This sun assumes all forms and has a golden color. He is called Jataveda, the all-knowing one. He is the goal, the primal light, and the source of heat. Moving in a hundred ways, this sun rises and gives life to beings with its thousand rays.'

9. "Prajapati, the creator and lord of creatures, became the year. He has two courses, a southern course and a northern course.[7] Those who think sacrifice and pious actions are what is most important follow the path to the moon, only to return to this world. Those sages who desire offspring and worldly prosperity

---

[7] Between December 21st and June 21st the sun moves in an apparent northerly direction along the horizon. This is called *uttarāyana*, moving north, and it is the path of light as the amount of daylight increases. From June 22nd to December 20th the amount of light decreases as the sun moves in a southerly direction along the horizon. This is called *dakṣiṇāyana*, moving south, and it is the path of darkness. Those who leave this world during the time of light attain the *ātmā* by way of the sun. Those who leave during the time of darkness attain the forefathers by way of the moon and eventually return to this earth.

[8] This verse is found in RV 1.164.12 and it describes a divinity who is both transcendent and immanent. The number references are obscure, but commentators suggest they refer to the seasons and the months.

[9] The lunar month is divided into two parts, a waxing part and a waning part. These are respectively called the *śukla-pakṣa* and *kṛṣṇa-pakṣa*.

follow this southern course. This is the *rayi* course that leads to the ancestors. It is the *lunar* path.

10. "Those who seek the *ātmā,* however, proceed by the northern course and, through their austerities, chastity and knowledge, attain the sun. This course indeed is the path to immortality and fearlessness. It is the highest shelter, and those who attain this state are no longer subject to rebirth. It is the final stoppage. In this regard there is the following verse:

11. "'Some call Him the Father with five feet and twelve parts who dwells on the far side of the sky. Some call Him the radiant One with seven wheels and six spoke who dwells on the near side of the sky.'[8]

12. "The creator Prajapati became the month with its two parts.[9] *Rayi* is the dark side, while *prāna* is the bright side. Therefore, true seers perform sacrifices only on the bright side of the month, while others do so on the dark side of the month.

13. "The creator Prajapati became day and night. Day is *prāṇa,* while night is *rayi*. Those who have sex during the daytime spill their life. Those who have sex during the night follow the rules of chastity.

14-16. "The creator Prajapati became food. Semen comes from food. Beings are born from food. So those who follow the vow of Prajapati produce a couple. Those who follow the path of austerity and chastity, which is founded on truth, own the world of *brahma*. Indeed, those who are free of duplicity, falsehood and deceit own that stainless world of *brahma!"*

Here ends the First *Praśna*

Second *Praśna*

1. Bhargava Vaidarbhi then approached the sage Pippalada and asked, "Good Sir, how many gods does it take to support the life of beings? Which one shines the most and which one is the most prominent?"

2. Pippalada replied, "Space[10] is one such divinity,[11] along with wind, fire, earth, speech, mind, eye and ear. Standing radiant, they all declared, 'We uphold and support this reed.'[12]

---

[10] The word is *ākāśa,* and it refers to space as the distance between points.

[11] The word is *deva,* which means a god. It is derived from the root *div,* meaning to shine. Here the elements of nature, such as wind and fire, along with the senses are considered gods or shining ones.

[12] The word is *bāṇu,* which is a reed or shaft, like an arrow. Here it means the body.

[13] There are five life-breaths: *prāṇa, apāna, vyāna, udāna* and *samāna.* See BU 1.3.3-5. See also, below, PU 3.5.

[14] That is to say, breath started to leave the body.

[15] The Sanskrit actually says "king-bee," *madhu-kara-rājanam*. It appears that the queen bee in a hive was considered to be male and so the reference to king-bee.

3. "But then life-breath, *prāṇa,* stood up and said, 'Do not be fooled by what the others say. I am the most prominent. As I divide myself five ways,[13] I uphold and support this reed.'

"But they did not believe him.

4. "With a certain pride, *prāṇa* then rose up from the body.[14] Immediately all the senses rose up and, when *prāṇa* sat down, they all sat down. It is just like bees who follow their queen.[15] When she flies off, they fly off. When she returns, they return. So speech, mind, eye and ear all do the same. They realized the truth of this and praised *prāṇa*.

5. "*Prāṇa* burns as fire; it is the sun. It is rain; it is bounty. It is wind; it is earth; it is shining matter. It is being and non-being. It is immortality.

6. "As the spokes of a wheel are tied to the hub, so all things, including the Rig, Yajur, and Sama Vedas, along with sacrifice, the *brāhmana* and the *kṣatriya,* are all fixed to *prāṇa*.

7. "O Life-breath, as lord of all creatures you move within the womb and it is you who are born. It is you who resides with the organs of the body. Therefore, all beings bring you tribute.

8. "You are the chief bearer of offerings to the gods. You are the first offering to the ancestors. You are the penance of the sages who are followers of Atharvan and Angiras.

9. "O Life-breath, by your radiance you are Indra; as the guardian you are Rudra. As the sun you move in space, you are the Lord of all light.

10. "O Life-breath, when you send forth the rains all creatures feel joy, thinking there will be as much food as we desire!

11. "O Life-breath, you are the most pure,[16] the primal one, and the consumer and lord of all things. We honor you with food offerings. O Matarishvan, you are our father.

---

[16] The word is *vrātya,* which refers to a high caste man who has lost his caste status due to the non performance of ritual duties, such as the thread-ceremony and the daily prayers associated with that rite. But here, since *prāṇa* was the first, there was no one to administer these rites; therefore he is called *vrātya*. Here, however, the meaning is not of a fallen person due to the lack of rites.

[17] There are five forms of *prāṇa: vyāna, samāna, udāna, prāṇa* and *apāna.*

[18] The word is *ati-praśna. Praśna* is "question" and the prefix *ati* adds increase. This can be taken as too many questions or very good questions, or even difficult questions.

[19] This is the answer to the first question, "What is the source of *prāṇa?"*

[20] The word is *chāyā*, which is a shadow or shade, or even a reflected image. Here it refers to the subtle astral body, sometimes called the *liṅga-śarīra.*

[21] This is the answer to the second question, "How does it enter the body?"

[22] This verse and the following two verses answer the third question, "How does it function within the body?"

12. "Your presence pervades our speech, our hearing, sight, and all our thoughts. Make them auspicious. Do not leave us.

13. "You pervade and control the three worlds through your life-breath. As a mother protects her children, protect us and grant us beauty and wisdom."

Here Ends the Second *Praśna*

Third *Praśna*

1. Kausalya Ashvalayana then asked the sage Pippalada the following question: "Kind Sir, what is the source of *prāṇa*, life-breath? How does it enter this body? Having divided itself,[17] how does it function within the body? How does it leave the body? What is it called when it is outside the body and what is it called when it is inside the body?"

2. Pippalada replied, "You ask many questions[18] and because you are devoted to *brahma,* I will answer.

3. "*Prāṇa* arises from the soul.[19] Just as a shadow spreads out from a body, so the mind creates a 'shadow body'[20] by which this *prāṇa* enters the next body.[21]

4. "As a king appoints ministers saying, 'You take care of these villages, you take care of these other villages,' so *prāṇa* divides himself into different breaths and assigns them their respective places within the body.[22]

5. "The breath known as *apāna* resides at the organs of elimination and generation. The breath known as *prāṇa* moves itself through the mouth and the nose and resides at the eye and the ear. The breath known as *samāna* resides at the middle region

---

[23] Fire is said to have seven tongues. See MundU 1.2.4.

[24] There are other Upanishadic references to these pathways called *nāḍis.* See BU 1.2.19.

[25] This is the answer to the fourth question, "How does it leave the body?" Good deeds are called *puṇya* and bad deeds are called *pāpa. Puṇya* leads to a heaven and *pāpa* leads to a hell. There are seven heavens above earth and seven hells below earth. None are permanent. When a being in a heaven "spends away" his *puṇya,* he returns to earth. When a being in a hell "burns off" his *pāpa,* he returns to earth.

[26] This verse answers the final two questions: "What is *prāṇa* called when it is outside the body and what is it called when it is inside the body?" *Prāṇa* has its manifestation in both the external world as well as in the internal physical body. The physical is controlled by the cosmic.

[27] The breath known as *apāna* manifests in the external realm as the earth, which supports and holds up all things. Sometimes it is compared to gravity. In the body, as noted above, it is found in the lower region and manifests as the organs of elimination and generation.

[28] In the external world, the "space between" is the space between the earth and heaven. In the internal world of the body, the "space between" is the area of the stomach where digestion takes place.

[29] *Prāṇa* manifests in the outside world as wind. This same *prāṇa* in the inside world is breath.

[30] This verse describes the process of rebirth. According to the state of consciousness one develops in one's current life, one attains an appropriate new birth. See BG 8.6.

of the body and digests what has been eaten by becoming the seven fires.[23]

6. "The *ātmā* resides at the heart, where there are a hundred and one veins and arteries. Each of them branch into a hundred more, which in turn branch into seventy-two thousand more, The breath known as *vyāna* travels along these veins and arteries.[24]

7. "Through these pathways the breath known as *udāna* moves a person who has performed good deeds to a higher world and a person who has performed bad deeds to a lower world. Persons who have performed both good and bad deeds return to the world of men.[25]

8. "*Prāṇa* manifests in the external world as the sun, Aditya, who rises and favors the *prāṇa* that manifests as the eye and sight.[26] The same *prāṇa* manifests as the earth deity, who becomes the breath known as *apāna* in man.[27] The space between is the breath known as *samāna*.[28] The wind is controlled by the breath known as *vyāna*.[29]

9-10. "The breath known as *udāna* is the fire of life. When that fire is extinguished, the senses and the mind merge and one is reborn into this world. According to how one is thinking at the time of death, one merges with the life-breath and, together with fire and the *ātmā,* one is led to whatever world has been fashioned by thought.[30]

11. "The learned person who understands this life-breath (*prāṇa)* does not lose his offspring and soon becomes immortal. In this regard there is the following verse:

---

[31] Five questions are asked. These questions refer to four states of consciousness: sleeping, waking, dreaming, and dreamless sleep.

[32] Here the word is *deva,* which means a god, but here it is used for the senses of the body, which are considered "gods." The root of the word is *div,* meaning to shine. Therefore, a *deva* is literally a shining one. Thus, the senses are the "shining ones" in the context of the body.

[33] This is the answer to the first question, "Who is it that sleeps?" The answer is it is the body and the senses that sleep in ordinary sleep.

[34] Here, of course, the fort is the physical body. The word used here is *prāṇāgnayah,* the fires of breath. *Prāṇa* is the general term used for breath. This prāṇa divides itself into five sub-breaths known as *apāna, vyāna* and *prāṇa, samāna* and *udāna.* (Note: The word *prāṇa* is used in two ways, for the general term "breath" and as a sub-breath.)

[35] Traditionally, a householder, who was a member of the three upper *varṇas*, would maintain a fire in the home at all times. This was the western fire, called the *gārhapatya* fire or the householder's fire. This fire was to be kept burning at all times and was even passed down from father to son. The second fire was the southern fire, called the *anvāhāryapacana* fire, and the third was the eastern fire, called the *āhavanīya* fire or the offertorial fire. The western *gārhapatya* fire was maintained by daily offerings and, at the time of major rituals, the other fires were lighted from this *gārhapatya* fire. The southern fire was used for offerings to the ancestors, while the eastern fire was for the gods. Life itself was seen as a sacrifice; therefore, these three fires are symbolically identified as these sub-breaths.

12. "One who knows the origins of *prāṇa*, its entrance into the body, how it resides at the various organs, how it divides itself fivefold, and how it relates to the external and internal worlds attains immortality. Indeed, such a person attains immortality!"

Here Ends the Third *Praśna*

Fourth *Praśna*

1. Next Sauryayani Gargya asked the sage Pippalada the following questions:[31] "Good Sir, who is it that sleeps? Who is it that is awake? Who is the god[32] who sees in dreams? Who experiences the joy of deep sleep? And on what does all this hang?"

2. Pippalada replied, "It is just like, when the sun sets, the rays are pulled back into a single orb, and then, when it rises again, all those same rays burst forth. Similarly, O Gargya, when a person experiences sleep, his consciousness is pulled back and becomes one in that supreme faculty of the mind only to burst forth once again when he awakens. For this reason, when a person no longer hears, sees, smells, tastes, touches, speaks, enjoys, evacuates or moves, we say he is sleeping.[33]

3. "The fires of breath burn in this fort.[34] The breath known as *apāna* is the *gārhapatya* fire, the householder's fire.[35] The breath known as *vyāna* is the southern *anvāhāryapacana* fire, and the breath known as *prāṇa* is the eastern *āhavanīya* fire, which is taken from the householder's *gārhapatya* fire.

4. "The sub-breath known as *samāna* is so named because it links[36] the two other sub-breaths, inhalation and exhalation. The mind is indeed the patron of the sacrifice. The fruit of the sacrifice is the breath known as *udāna*, which leads the sacrificer into the deep sleep of *brahma*.[37]

---

[36] Literally, "leads to sameness." The word *sama,* out of which *samāna* is formed, means sameness. Here inhalation and exhalation are linked together or made the same by the breath known as *samāna*. These breaths here are considered oblations into the fire.

[37] Verses 3 and 4 answer the second question, "Who is it that is awake?" The answer is *prāṇa.* It is *prāṇa* that maintains the body during wakefulness. See also CU 6.8.1-2, wherein it is stated that breath is the tether of the mind.

[38] This verse answers the third question, "Who is the god that sees in dreams?" The answer is the mind.

[39] In a dream the dreamer generally sees himself as the "hero" of his own story; therefore, the verse says he experiences glory.

[40] "Whatever has been seen or not seen": "Not seen" means whatever has been seen in a previous life. "He himself is all" means that, through multiple lifetimes, the soul has experienced all things and in this sense is all things.

[41] The word is *tejas*, which is literally heat or light. Here we take it as the light of *brahma*.

[42] The person who focuses on *brahma* gradually fills himself with "*brahma* light." His sleep is deep and dreamless as he increasingly touches *brahma*. When he awakens he is filled with great joy. This is the answer to the fourth question.

[43] Verses 7 to 9 answer the fifth question, "On what does all this hang?" The answer is the supreme *ātmā*.

5. "In sleep this god[38] experiences glory.[39] He sees in dreams whatever he sees in wakefulness. He hears in dreams whatever he hears in wakefulness. He experiences in dreams whatever he experiences in different places and from different regions. Whatever has been seen or not seen, whatever has been heard or not heard, whatever has been experienced or not experienced, whatever is real or unreal—he sees it all because he himself is all.[40]

6. "Indeed, as this god becomes filled with light,[41] he no longer experiences dreams. Instead he experiences the great happiness or *brahma*.[42]

7. As nesting birds find shelter in a tree, my child, so all this world finds shelter in that supreme *ātmā*.[43]

8. "The earth and its elements, water and its elements, fire and its elements, wind and its elements, space and its elements, the eye and what is seen, the ear and what is heard, the nose and what is smelled, taste and what is tasted, the skin and what is touched, speech and what is spoken, the hands and what is handled, the organ of generation and the pleasure it produces, the organ of evacuation and what is evacuated, the feet and where one goes, the mind and what is thought, the intellect and what is intellectualized, one's identity and what is experienced as oneself, perception and what can be perceived, light and what can be illuminated, and life-breath and what it can support—all these take shelter of that supreme *ātmā*.

9. "This one who sees, this one who touches, this one who hears,

smells, tastes, thinks and acts, is the conscious person who takes shelter of that supreme imperishable *ātmā*.

10. "Indeed, he who comes to know that supreme radiant one who has no shadow, no body or blood, becomes omniscient. He understands that he is all things. In this regard there is the following verse.

11. "'The conscious soul, breath, and all the elements, along with the senses,[44] rest on the imperishable. The one who knows this, my child, himself becomes omniscient and enters all things.'"

Here Ends the Fourth *Praśna*

Fifth *Praśna*

1. Next Shaibya Satyakama asked the sage Pippalada the following question: "Good Sir, if a person's spiritual practice in-

---

[44] The words are *saha devaiś ca sarvaiḥ,* "along with all *devas*." Here *deva* has been contextually rendered as "the senses."

[45] The syllable *om* is here broken down into three sounds: *a, u, m*.

[46] Literally, "What world does he win?"

[47] See MU 1.1.4, where higher *brahma* knowledge is said to be knowledge of the imperishable *brahma,* while lower *brahma* knowledge is defined as practical or worldly knowledge found in the Vedas. Similarly, the Isha Upanishad talks about two forms of knowledge, *vidyā* and *avidyā* which may be described as spiritual and secular knowledge.

volves meditation on the syllable *om*[45] until death, what is his ultimate destination?"[46]

2. To Shaibya Satyakama Pippalada replied, "Satyakama, the sound *om* represents both the higher and the lower forms of *brahma*.[47] Therefore a learned person, who understands this, can obtain either result.

3. "If a person meditates on only one syllable of *om*, the *a*, which is to say if his spiritual practice is incomplete, he quickly becomes enlightened to that extent and attains this world, so that after passing he is carried by Rig mantras back to this world of men, where he experiences greatness due to his past austerities, chastity and faith.

4. "If a person meditates on the two syllables of *om*, the *a* and *u,* which is to say if his spiritual practice is more complete yet still not mature, he is led by Yajur mantras to the region of the sky wherein he attains the moon. After enjoying there in the lunar world, he returns to earth.

5. "When one has meditated on that supreme person using the three syllables of *om* (*a, u, m*), which is to say when one's spiritual practice is complete, that person attains the light of the sun. And just as a snake sheds its skin, so one becomes freed from evil and is led by the Sama mantras to *brahma-loka*, the realm of *brahma*. There one sees that Supreme Person who dwells within the body and who is higher than the highest. In this regard there are two verses:

6. "'When they are joined together and not separated, the three syllables of *om* lead to immortality.[48] When these syllables are properly employed in the external, internal and intermediate states,[49] a learned person experiences no fear in this world.'

7. "'Through Rig verses one attains this world, through Yajur verses one attains the intermediate regions, and through Sama verses one attains the supreme realm that mystics proclaim. Through the employment of the sound *om,* the learned attain the realm of peace, which is the highest state, beyond old age, death and fear.'"

Here Ends the Fifth *Praśna*

Sixth *Praśna*

1. Next Sukesha Bharadvaja spoke the following to the sage

---

[48] This line can also be read as "The three syllables of *om*, if employed separately, lead to rebirth."

[49] Waking, dreaming sleep and deep sleep.

[50] The sixteen parts are listed in verse 4 below. In both the BU (1.5.15) and CU (6.7) and elsewhere, the body is said to be composed of sixteen parts.

[51] The "he" here is *prāṇa,* life-breath. See above, PU 2.3-4.

[52] The pure soul (*puruṣa*) enters this world and becomes "mixed" with matter, *prakṛti,* and together this pure soul, along with *prakṛti*/matter, create a body made of sixteen parts. The main constituent of that body is *prāṇa.* The *prāṇa* is supreme. When it leaves the body, everything else also leaves. When it stays, everything else stays.

Pippalada: "Good Sir, once Hiranyanabha, a prince from the kingdom of Koshala, came to me and asked the following question, 'O Bharadvaja, do you know the *puruṣa* with sixteen parts?'[50]

"I replied to this young man: 'I do not know this *puruṣa*, but, if I did know, I would surely tell you, for a person who lies withers to the root. Therefore, I cannot lie.'

"This prince then quietly got into his chariot and drove away. So now I ask you the same question: O Great Sage, who is that *puruṣa* with sixteen parts?"

2. The sage Pippalada replied, "Dear friend, the *puruṣa* from whom the sixteen parts arise dwells right here in this body.

3. "That *puruṣa* then reflected: When he[51] departs, I depart, and when he stays, I stay. Who is this one?

4. "The *puruṣa* first creates life-breath, and from life-breath comes faith, space, wind, light, waters, earth, the senses, mind and food; and from food there comes virility, heat, prayers, actions, the worlds and, in the world, names.[52]

5. "As rivers flow towards the ocean and, upon arriving, merge into that ocean, losing their name and form and so are called simply "ocean," so that seer[53] with sixteen parts flows toward the *puruṣa*[54] and upon arriving, merges into that *puruṣa* and so loses his name and form and so is simply called *puruṣa*. Having

no parts, he becomes immortal.

In this regard there is the following verse:

6. "'You must know this *puruṣa,* who alone must be known and in whom these parts are fixed like the spokes of a chariot wheel are firmly attached to its hub. In this way you will not be disturbed by death.'"

7. The sage Pippalada then said to them, "This is as much as I know about this supreme *brahma*. There is nothing more to be known."

8. They thanked him and said, "You are truly our father because you have brought us to the farthest shore beyond ignorance. Respects to the highest seers. Respects to the highest seers!"

Thus ends the Sixth *Praśna*
Thus ends the Prashna Upanishad

---

[53] That seer is the *puruṣa.* In a sense there are two *puruṣa,* the individual *puruṣa* and the supreme *puruṣa,* or, in later language, the *jīvātmā* and the *paramātmā*, the soul and the super soul. The analogy is that the *paramātmā* is like a gold mine and the *jīvātmā* is like a nugget from that mine. They are the same and yet different. In this case the seer is the *jīvātmā puruṣa.*

[54] Here the *puruṣa* referred to is the *paramātmā puruṣa.* So when the *jīvātmā puruṣa* returns to the *paramātmā puruṣa,* it merges and loses its outward form like a river returning to the ocean.

10
Mandukya Upanishad

Introduction to

Mandukya Upanishad

The Mandukya Upanishad is generally assigned to the Atharva Veda. It is the smallest of the Upanishads, with only twelve verses that deal with the sacred syllable *om*, which it identifies with the world, *brahma*, and the *ātmā*. The three constituent phonemes of the syllable *om* (*a, u, m*) are further identified with the four states of consciousness—the waking state, the dreaming state, the deep sleep state, and a mystical state. The historical importance of the Mandukya Upanishad is dependent on the famous commentary or Karika by Gaudapada, who was the grand guru of Shankaracharya, the great exponent of monistic philosophy (Advaita Vedanta).

Om and the Four States of Awareness

1. The sound *om* encompasses all things. *Om* includes the past, the present, and the future and indeed, whatever is beyond these three is also *om*.

2. *Brahma* encompasses all things. *Ātmā* is *brahma*. This *ātmā* has four states[1] of awareness.

3. The first state is called "universal."[2] It is the waking state wherein one perceives and enjoys this coarse external world. It has seven limbs and nineteen faces.[3]

---

[1] The word is *pāda*, which is literally a "foot," and by extension means a quarter. Here the word has been glossed to mean the four states of awareness that are described in the following verses.

[2] The word is *vaiśvānara*, "the universal," and it refers to the physical body, called the *sthula-śarira.* It is "universal" because all beings in this world experience this state of awareness.

[3] The references to seven and nineteen are obscure, but contextually suggest the body with seven "limbs" which include the head, breath, arms, hands, torso, legs, and feet. The nineteen "faces" are the organs that "light" up the body. They include the six organs of perception (ears, skin, eyes, tongue, nose and mind), five organs of action (mouth, hands, feet, penis and anus), the five breaths, intellect, ego, and consciousness.

4. The second state is called "luminous."[4] It is the dreaming state wherein one perceives and enjoys the subtle inner world. It too has seven limbs and nineteen faces.[5]

5-6. The third state is called "conscious."[6] It is the state wherein there is no desire and no dreaming. It is absolute deep sleep. In this state one's consciousness is unified and one loses all sense of external reality. It is a state characterized by consciousness alone, in which one experiences pure joy. This is the Lord of

---

[4] The word is *taijasa*, "the luminous," and it refers to the dream or astral body called the *sukṣma-śarira*.

[5] The astral body has all the components of the physical body, hence the seven "limbs" and the nineteen "faces."

[6] The word is *prājña,* "the conscious," and it refers to a state of concentrated awareness wherein one ceases to be aware of anything outside of this state.

[7] In the sound *om,* the *o* is a diphthong composed of the syllables *a* plus *u*. The syllables *a, u* and *m* represent the three states of awareness respectively: the awake state, the dreaming state, and deep sleep. All three syllables together make the combined sound *om,* which represents the fourth state of absolute absorption.

[8] The word is *vaiśvānara*, "universal." Waking consciousness is universal, or common to all beings.

[9] The word is *taijasa*, "made of light." Dreaming consciousness is luminous.

[10] The word is *prājña,* "cognition." Basically this refers to the *vijñāna-maya-kośa,* the intellect-body, mentioned in the Taittiriya Upanishad. It is this intellect-body that is best suited to contact the *ātmā.*

all, the omniscient One, the inner Soul, the source of all, the beginning and end of all beings.

7. They describe a fourth state of awareness, which is characterized by no inner or outer cognition, nor any combination of the two. In this state there is no cognition or even non-cognition. It is a state which is unseen, beyond all ordinary dealings, ungraspable, without characteristics, and beyond thought. It is indescribable. The essence of this state is the pure perception of the *ātmā,* wherein the physical world has ceased to exist. It is a state full of peace and beauty, and it is nondual.

8. This *ātmā* can be analyzed according to the syllables of *om*. The states of *ātmā* are reflected in the syllables *a*, *u*, and *m*.[7]

9. The first syllable, *a,* represents the waking state that is common to all.[8] It is from *āp,* "to obtain", and from *ādimattvā*, "being first." One who understand this fulfills all desires and becomes first among men.

10. The second syllable, *u,* represents the dreaming state defined as luminous.[9] It is from *utkarśaṇa, "exultation,"* and *ubhayatva,* "being in between." It gives rise to knowledge and equanimity. One who understands this will never have someone born into his lineage who does not know *brahma*.

11. The third syllable, *m,* represents the state of deep sleep characterized by pure consciousness.[10] It is from *miti*, "expanding"

and *apīti,* "contracting."[11] One who understands this is able to know how one's life expands and contracts.

12. The fourth state is without any syllables and so has no interaction with this world. It is a total withdrawal from this world. It is wholly auspicious and non-dual. In this way, the word *om* connects to the *ātmā,* and one who understands this enters the *ātmā* through the intellect.[12]

Thus ends the Mandukya Upanishad

---

[11] *Miti* is from the root *mā,* which means to "measure out" or "construct." *Apīti* is from *āp,* meaning to "absorb." Together the words suggest the expansion and contraction of one's existence. One who can enter this third state of awareness is able to see the expansion, or rolling out, of his existence and thereby is also able to absorb back or roll back his life in this world.

[12] The words are *samviśaty ātmanā 'ātmanam,* literally "he enters the *ātmā* by means of the *ātmā.*" The word *ātmā,* as noted many times has numerous meanings, two of which are intellect and mind. Mental discipline is essential for meditation. Therefore *ātmanā* has been rendered here as "by the intellect."

Sanskrit Glossary

ācārya–traditional teacher or theologian of Hindu doctrine, head of *sampradāya* or school of religious thought.

adharma–the opposite of *dharma*. The term is often used in the sense of unrighteousness, impiety or non-performance of duty.

adhibhūta–the manifestation of *brahma* as the perishable nature of matter.

adhidaiva–the manifestation of *brahma* as the Universal Person or *puruṣa* who is the foundation of the gods.

adhiyajña–the principle of divinity that dwells within all things and is the recipient of all sacrifice.

adhyātmā–the manifestation of *brahma* as the individual soul.

advaita–non dualism, the name given to the theological position of the Shankara school of thought.

agni–fire or the fire deity.

ahimsā–nonviolence.

akṣara–something that is imperishable, the soul, God.

āryan–one of noble birth, one faithful to the religion of the Vedas.

artha–wealth, not to be understood solely as material assets, but all kinds of wealth including non-tangibles such as knowledge, friendship and love. *Artha* is one of the four *puruṣārthas* or "goals of life," the others being *dharma*, *kāma* and *mokṣa*.

āśrama–one of the four stages of life: *brahmacarya* (studentship), *gārhasthya* (householder), *vānaprastha* (retired), and *sannyāsa* (renounced); a hermitage.

asat–opposite of *sat,* non-being, impermanent, false, evil, unreal, some- times used to refer to matter or to the body.

asura–an ungodly one, a demon, one who does not follow the path of the Vedas.

ātman–has many meanings in Sanskrit that include: soul, breath, the Self, one's self (as a reflexive pronoun), mind, body, the Supreme Soul, etc.

avatāra–literally, one who descends, an incarnation of God who descends into this physical world, an incarnation of Viṣṇu.

avidyā–non knowledge, ignorance, nescience.

bhagavān–literally, one possessed of *bhaga. Bhaga* means fame, glory, strength, power, etc. The word is used as an epithet applied to God, gods, or any holy or venerable personality.

bhakta–a devotee, one who follows the path of devotion.

bhakti–love, devotion. One of the most common forms of *yoga.*

bhakti-yoga–the spiritual path of connecting one's self to God through devotion.

brahmā–the four headed creator god born of the lotus.

brahmacārī–a religious student in the first stage of life.

brahmacarya–the first stage of life, studentship, celibacy.

brahman–derived from the Sanskrit root *bṛmh* meaning to grow, to expand, to bellow, to roar. The word *brahman* refers to the Supreme Principle regarded as impersonal and divested of all qualities. *Brahman* is the essence from which all created beings are produced and into which they are absorbed. This word is neuter and not to be confused with the masculine word Brahmā, the creator god. *Brahman* is sometimes used to denote the syllable *om* or the *Vedas* in general.

brāhmaṇa–a member of the traditional priestly class. The *brāhmaṇa* was the first of the four *varṇas* in the social system called *varṇāśrama- dharma.* Literally, the word means "in relation to brahman." A *brāhmaṇa* is one who follows the ways of *brahman.* Traditionally a *brāhmaṇa,* often written as brahmin, filled the role of priest, teacher and thinker.

candra–the moon or the moon deity.

deva–derived from the Sanskrit root *div* meaning to shine or become bright. A *deva* is therefore a "shining one." The word is used to refer to God, a god or any exalted personality. The female version is *devī.*

devanāgarī–name of the writing script in which Sanskrit and Hindi are usually written.

dharma–derived from the Sanskrit root *dhṛ* meaning to hold up, to carry, to bear, to sustain. The word *dharma* refers to that which upholds or sustains the universe. Human society, for example, is sustained and upheld by the *dharma* performed by its members. Parents protecting and maintaining children, children being obedient to parents, the king protecting the citizens are acts of *dharma* that uphold and sustain society. In this context *dharma* has the meaning of duty. *Dharma* also employs the meaning of law, religion, virtue, and ethics. These things uphold and sustain the proper functioning of human society. In philosophy *dharma* refers to the defining quality of an object. For instance, liquidity is one of the essential *dharmas* of water; coldness is a *dharma* of ice. In this case we can think that the existence of an object is sustained or defined by its essential attributes, *dharmas.*

duḥkha–suffering or unhappiness.

dvaita–dualism, the name given to the theological position of the Mādhva school of thought.

dvāpara-yuga–the third time period (*yuga*) said to last 864,000 years (two times 432,000)

gaṅgā–the river Ganges.

gārhasthya–the third order (*āśrama*) of life, domestic affairs.

gāyatrī–a meter used throughout the Vedas comprised of three lines of eight measures totaling twenty-four measures. A sacred chant.

guṇa–quality, positive attributes or virtues. In the context of *Bhagavad* Gītā and *Sāṅkhya* philosophy there are three *guṇas* of matter. Sometimes *guṇa* is translated as phase or mode. Therefore the three *guṇas* or phases of matter are: *sattva-guṇa*, *rajo-guṇa* and *tamo- guṇa*. The word *guṇa* also means a rope or thread and it is sometimes said that beings are "roped" or "tied" into matter by the three *guṇas* of material nature.

gṛhastha–one situated in the second order of life (*āśrama*), a householder.

guru–a teacher. Literally, the word means heavy and so refers to one "heavy" with knowledge, commonly used to refer to a spiritual teacher.

haṭha-yoga–a path of physical discipline meant to control the senses.

Īśā–literally, lord, master, or controller. *Īśā* is one of the words used for God as the supreme controller. The word is also used to refer to any being or personality who is in control.

Īśvara–see Īśā.

japa–chanting.

jīva–the soul, a living being.

jñāna–derived from the Sanskrit root *jñā*, to know, to learn, to experience. In the context of *Bhagavad Gītā* and the *Upaniṣads*, *jñāna* is generally used in the sense of spiritual knowledge or awareness.

jñāna-yoga–the spiritual path of connecting one's self to God through knowledge.

jñānī–literally, "one possessed of knowledge," a scholar.

kāma–wish, desire, love. Often used in the sense of sexual desire or love, but not necessarily. *Kāma* is one of the four *puruṣārthas* or "goals of life," the others being *dharma, artha* and *mokṣa.*

kāla–time.

kali-yuga–one of the four ages, said to last 432,000 years, the age characterized by fighting and diminished spiritual abilities.

kalpa–sacred law, a period of time, a twelve hour period (a day) of Brahmā said to last one thousand *mahā-yuga* cycles.

karma–derived from the Sanskrit root *kṛ* meaning to do, to make. The work *karma* means action, work, and deed. Only secondarily does *karma* refer to the result of past deeds, which are more properly known as the *phalam* or fruit of action.

karma-yoga–the spiritual path of connecting one's self to God through action or work.

kṣatriya–a member of the traditional military or warrior class. A king, a prince. The *kṣatriya* was the second *varṇa* in the system of *varṇāśrama-dharma.*

kṣara–something that is perishable, the body, the world.

kṣetra–a field, the body, the world.

kṣetra-jña–the knower of the field, the soul, God.

līlā–divine pastime, play of God.

mahā-yuga–a period of time comprised of one cycle of the four *yugas: satya, tretā, dvāpara* and *kali*, a total of 4,320,000 years.

mantra–a Vedic hymn or sacred prayer.

māyā–a trick, illusion.

mokṣa–liberation or freedom of rebirth. *Mokṣa* is one of the four *puruśārthas* or "goals of life," the others being *dharma,* *artha* and *kāma*.

mukti–see *mokṣa*.

muni–a sage, a silent one.

nirguṇa–without attributes, refers to God conceived to be impersonal.

nirvāṇa–blown out or extinguished as in the case of a lamp. *Nirvāṇa* is generally used to refer to a material life that has been extinguished, one who has achieved freedom from re-birth. The term *nirvāṇa* is commonly used in Buddhism as the final stage a practitioner strives for. The word does not mean heaven.

om–a sacred syllable, the sound of *brahman*, a sound vibrated at the beginning and end of Vedic recitation, the Vedas.

pāpa–literally, *pāpa* is what brings one down. Sometimes translated as sin or evil.

paramātman–the supreme soul, the supersoul, the lord of the heart, an aspect of God that pervades all things.

paramparā–one following the other, the chain of teachers and disciples.

pitṛ–a father, a forefather, an ancestor, a class of celestial beings, the manes.

prakṛti–material nature. In *sāṅkhya* philosophy *prakṛti* is comprised of eight elements: earth, water, fire, air, space, mind, intellect and ego. It is characterized by the three *guṇas*: *sattva*, *rajas* and *tamas*. *Prakṛti* is female. *Puruṣa* is male.

prāṇa–breath, life force, the senses.

prasāda–favor, mercy, blessing, God's blessings, any item that has been offered to God during worship, especially food.

puṇya–the opposite to *pāpa*. *Puṇya* is what elevates; it is virtue or moral merit. *Pāpa* and *puṇya* go together as negative and positive "credits." One reaps the reward of these negative or positive credits in life. The more *puṇya* one cultivates the higher one rises in life, whereas *pāpa* will cause one to find a lower position. *Puṇya* leads to happiness, *pāpa* leads to suffering.

puruṣa–man, male. In *sāṅkhya* philosophy *puruṣa* denotes the Supreme Male Principle in the universe. Its counterpart is *prakṛti.*

puruṣottama–comprised of two words: *puruṣa* + *uttama* literally meaning "highest man." *Puruṣottama* means God.

rajas–the second of the three *guṇas* of matter. Sometimes translated as passion, the phase of *rajas* is characterized by action, passion, creation, etc.

ṛta–what is proper, right, true, divine law.

ṛtu–season, a period of time, menstruation period.

ṛṣi–an inspired poet or sage, a class of beings distinct from men and gods who were the "seers" of the Vedas.

saṅkhya–calculating, enumeration, analysis, categorization. Modern science can be said to be a form of *saṅkhya* because it attempts to analyze and categorize matter into its constituent elements. *Sāṅkhya* (first *a* long) refers to an ancient system of philosophy attributed to the sage Kapila. This philosophy is so called because it enumerates or analyses reality into a set number of basic elements, similar to modern science.

saguṇa–literally, "with attributes," God conceived as possessing humanlike qualities.

śaiva–a follower of Śiva.

śākta–a follower of Durgā (*śakti*).

śakti–power, energy conceived as female in nature.

samādhi–meditative trance, absorption in the divine.

sannyāsī–one situated in the final stage (*āśrama*) of life, a mendicant.

sannyāsa–the fourth or final stage (*āśrama*) of life, characterized by full renunciation.

śāstra–an order, command, rule, scriptural injunction, sacred writings, science, any department of knowledge.

sat–being, good, virtuous, chaste, the third word of the famous three words: *oṃ tat sat,* refers to what is truly real, eternal and permanent, used to mean God or the soul.

sattva–the first of the three *guṇas* of matter. Sometimes translated as goodness, the phase of *sattva* is characterized by lightness, peace, cleanliness, knowledge, etc.

satyam–truth. The word *satyam* is formed from *sat* with the added abstract suffix *ya*. *Sat* refers to what is true and real. The abstract suffix *ya* means "ness." Thus *satyam* literally means trueness or realness.

satya-yuga–the first of the four *yugas*, said to comprise 1,728,000 years, characterized by virtue, wisdom and spirituality.

śloka–a hymn or verse of praise, a stanza or verse in general, a stanza in *anuṣṭubh* metre (the most common metre used in Sanskrit consisting for 4 lines of 8 syllables), fame.

smṛti–literally, "what is heard," the division of the Vedas written by human beings (*pauruṣeya*), comprised of the later tradition that includes the *Mahābhārata*, *Rāmāyana*, *Purāṇas* etc.

śruti–literally, "what is heard," the division of the Vedas not written by human beings (*apauruṣeya*), said to be "heard" by the *ṛṣis*, comprised of the four Vedas including the *Upaniṣads*.

śūdra–a member of the traditional working class. The śūdra was the fourth *varṇa* in the system of *varṇāśrama-dharma*.

sukha–happiness, pleasure.

sura–a godly one, a god, one who follows the path of the Vedas.

svāmī–controller, a *yogī*, one in the renounced stage of life, a *guru*.

tamas–the third of the three *guṇas* of matter. Sometimes translated as darkness, the phase of *tamas* is characterized by darkness, ignorance, slowness, destruction, heaviness, disease, etc.

tapas–heat, voluntary acceptance of trouble for a spiritual goal, austerity, penance.

tapasya–see *tapas*.

tretā-yuga–the second of the four *yugas*, said to last 1,296,000 years.

tyāga–abandonment, renunciation, the performance of actions without attachment to the results of action.

vaikuṇṭha–literally, "without anxiety," the realm or heaven of Viṣṇu.

vairāgya–renounciation, detachment from the world.

vaiṣṇava–a follower of Viṣṇu.

vaiśya–a member of the traditional mercantile or business community. The *vaiśya* was the third *varṇa* in the system of *varṇāśrama-dharma*.

vānaprastha–the third order (*āśrama*) of life, the retired stage. Literally, "one who remains in the forest."

varṇāśrama–the traditional social system of four *varṇas* and four *aśramas*. The word *varṇa* literally means, "color" and it refers to four basic natures of mankind: *brāhmaṇa*, *kṣatriya*, *vaiśya* and *śūdra*. The *āśramas* are the four stages of an individual's life: *brahmacarya* (student), *gṛhastha* (householder), *vanaprastha* (retired) and *sannyāsa* (renounced).

veda(s)–knowledge, the sacred knowledge of the āryans, the Hindu scriptures, the *Ṛg, Yajur, Sāma, Atharva*, the *Mahābhārata, Rāmāyaṇa, Purāṇas, Vedānta-sūtra,* etc.

vidyā–knowledge, the goddess Sarasvatī.

vijñāna–derived from the prefix *vi* added to the noun *jñāna*. The prefix *vi* added to a noun tends to diminish or invert the meaning of a word. If *jñāna* is spiritual knowledge, *vijñāna* is practical or profane knowledge. Sometimes *vijñāna* and *jñāna* are used together in the sense of knowledge and wisdom.

viśiṣṭādvaita–often translated as "oneness of the organic unity" or "differentiated monism," the theology taught by the Śrī Vaiṣṇavism associated with Rāmānuja.

viśva-rūpa–God's cosmic form, the universal form, the vision seen by Arjuna in *Bhagavad Gītā* Chapter Eleven.

yajña–sacrifice, the worship of God performed with fire.

yoga–derived from the Sanskrit root *yuj*, to join, to unite, to attach. The English word yoke is cognate with the Sanskrit word *yoga*. We can think of *yoga* as the joining of the *ātman* with the *paramātman*, the soul with God. There are numerous means of joining with God: through action, *karma-yoga*; through knowledge, *jñāna-yoga*; through devotion, *bhakti-yoga*; through meditation, *dhyāna-yoga*, etc. *Yoga* has many other meanings. For example, in astronomy and astrology it refers to a conjunction (union) of planets.

yogī–literally, one possessed of *yoga*. A *yogī* is a practitioner of *yoga*.

yuga–a period of time said to comprise 432,000 years, one of the four ages that rotate like calendar seasons.

Index

A

actions, 14, 128, 158, 188
  good and evil, 179
advaita, 116n, 140n, 162n, 206n
ancestors (forefathers), 14, 156n, 188-189, 196n
asat (unreal), xxviii-xxix, 22-23, 35n
astral body, 192n, 208n
ātmā (self, soul), 34-43, 107-121, 127-129, 136-142, 176-183, 206-210
austerity, 12-13, 27-28, 94, 143
avidyā, (ignorance), 103, 130-131, 156, 167n, 200n

B

boon, 69, 96
brahma, viii, xxi-xxvi, 17-31, 50, 55-57, 64-65, 88-93, 119-123, 175-183
Brahmā (creator god), viii, 50-55, 154n, 163, 167,
brāhmana, xxvii , 11, 86, 112, 191
breath, 9, 19, 28-31, 36, 65-67, 70-73, 190-200
  five breaths, 139
  seven breaths, 175
Brihaspati, 5, 15, 25, 51

C

Campbell, Joseph, xxvii
cognition, 43, 209
compassion, 139n
consciousness, 34, 43, 112n, 197, 206-210
creation, 34-37, 113, 159-160

D

Darwin, Charles, xix
death, 27-29, 35-38, 96-105, 111-117, 131-132
demons, 83
desire, 21-26, 55-59, 101-107, 139n, 181
dharma, 13, 105, 160
directions, 11, 36, 37, 150
disease, 145
dreams, 71, 80-82, 197-199
duality, 26

E

evil,
  actions, 179
  deeds, 50, 179
  destroyer of, 160
  freed from, 201
  untouched by, 130

eye, 35-40
  brahma, 180
  consciousness is, 43
  of introspection, 113
  prāṇa, 195
  protector, 55
  six organs of perception, 207
  sun, 118, 174

F

father,
  as a god, 14
  father-son ceremony, 67-69
  made of twelve parts, 49, 189
  rebirth, 34
fear,
  free of, 26, 202
  of *brahma,* 24, 119-120
  of old age, 99
fearless, 23, 189
fire sacrifice (*agni-hotra*), 8n, 58-59, 96, 99-100, 170-171, 196-197
forefathers, see ancestors
food, 29-32, 38-39
  container, 3, 176-177
  essence of mankind, 17-19
food-body, 18-19, 26
form, 35, 106
  embodied soul assumes, 157-159
  God exists in three, 146n
  gross and subtle, 187
  of *atma*, 112-114, 118, 141, 177
  of Creative Principle, 133
  of *Puruṣa*, 121
formless, 149

G

Gandharvas, 24-25, 121, 139
gāyatrī, 154n
gods,
  deva, 196
  happiness of, 25
  immortal, 67
  rites to, 14
  take the path of, 49
greatness, 159, 201

H

havan, see fire sacrifice
hearing, 10-11, 36-37, 66, 70-75
heart, 10, 63,
  atma, 107-109, 113-116, 195
High Chant, xxv, 51
homa, see fire sacrifice
honey-eater, 108, 112-113
horse, 37, 43,
  control mind, 145
  senses are, 109
human happiness, 24

I

ignorance (*avidyā*), 102n, 128n, 130-131, 139n, 171, 204

immortal,
  become, 87, 183
  gods are, 67
  person in the heart, 10
  prāṇa, 196-197
  puruṣa, 117
  vidyā, 156
immortality,
  attain, 121-123, 147-150
  brahma as, 31
  bridge to, 177-178
  door to, 140n
  finding, 89
  giver of, 160
  Indra as, 70
  obtained, 42-43
  om leads to, 202-204
  pathway to, 99, 112-113, 189
  prāṇa is, 191
  truth and, 176
  vidyā, 131-133
imperishable,
  ātmā, 151, 200
  brahma as, 106, 109, 173
  Brahmā, 166-169
Indra, 5, 10, 24-25,
  surpass other gods, 93

J

jīvātmā,
  deva as, 104n
  disentangle from *prakṛti*, 141n
  nature of, 146n
  puruṣa, 116n
  swan (*haṃsa*), 162n
  two kinds of *ātmās*, 108n, 112n, 114n, 152n, 160n, 204n
joy, 9-10
  brahma is, 29
  container, 3, 18, 21-23, 176n
  of procreation, 31, 54

K

King Soma, 61-62, 78, 82
knowledge (*vidyā*), 3, 6-7, **130-131**
  ātmā, 179-180
  avidyā (ignorance), 102n, 139n
  brahma is, 17
  find immortality, 89
  five senses, 121
  of *brahma*, 22, 143-144, 183, 200
  of fire sacrifice, 96
  knowledge-self, 111
  man of, 49-51
  prājñāna, 42n
  sacred, 69, 79-81
  Vedic, 163, 166-169
kuṇḍalinī, 144n

L

language, xxvi
lightning,
  brahma as, 31, 65
  flash of, 93

person in, 77-78
yogī, 145
law, 14, 20n, 116-117, 174

M

man,
creation of, 35-37, 203
death, 100
desire love of, 58
embryo, 41
form of, 19-21
high caste, 192n
learned in Vedas, 24-26
lose vital functions, 69-72
of knowledge, 49-52
puruṣa, 110n, 149n, 172n
seek to apprehend, 76
six organs of perception, 207
sleep, 197-199
soul return to earth, 174n
virility, 61-63
mankind,
from food, 17-18
māyā, xxix, 22n, 152n
meditation, 138, 142-143, 144n, 166, 176n, 180, 201, 210n
mind,
ātmā, 89, 158n, 210n
breath controls, 55-56
brahma is, 27-31
creation of, 36-37
enters next body, 193
essence, 107-111
fed by five streams, 138-140n
fully focused, 176
insight, 93
lord of, 10-11
mind-body, 18n, 20-21, 26
superior, 121
untrained horses, 145
vital function, 71-76
what drives the, 87
moon,
attain the, 201
creation, 36-37
essential element, 11
go to, 48-49
new, 57, 61, 170
path to, 188
person in, 78
Puruṣa, 174
shining, 65
mortal world, 101-102

N

nonexistence, 159
non-being, 35n, 130, 155, 191

O

oblations, 57, 144, 170, 198n
Om, 5, 11, 17, 133n, 142-143, 177, 202, 206-210

P

pāpa, 194n
paramātmā,
cosmic man, 148n
eternal and sentient, 160n
fire, 162n
higher soul, 108n
goldmine analogy, 204n
nature of, 146n
puruṣa, 152n
two forms of *ātmā*, 112n
shining one, 104n
size of thumb, 116n
super-soul, 140n
watches, 178n
path to *brahma*, 87-88
path of sacrifice, 88-89, 103
power, 49-51, 95-96, 144-145
Prajapati,
chant of, 42-44
Lord of Creatures, 168-176
offspring, 32
sound *hiṃ*, 24
the creator, 89
prāṇa (life force), 4-7, 59, 82n, 94n, 96n, 111
procreate, 66n

R

rasa, 18n, 22n, 23
real, see *sat*
religion of affirmation, xxvii-xxviii
restraint, 94

S

Sānkhya philosophy, 20n, 110n, 138n
sat (real), xxviii-xxix, 23, 35n, 52, 88n, 178n
sattva (goodness), 138n, 152n, 158n
semen, 34, 36-37, 40-41, 49, 138n, 174n, 180n, 189
sleep,
dreams, 71, 80-82
states of consciousness, 196-199
three kinds of, 39-40
Smith, Wilford Cantwell, xviii
soma, 51, 144
soul, see *jīvātmā*,
body and, 140-145
caged to physical body, 42n
deny the, 128
embodied, 157-162
inner *puruṣa*, 149-152
of All, 107-109, 112-121
of every being, 52
mind-body, 19-21
sun,
brahma is, 26, 31, 152
essential element, 9-11

eye of the worlds, 118, 174
is *prāṇa*, 187-189, 191-192, 195
rises, 24, 60
shining, 64
sight, 36-37
sun (continued)
surveyor of all, 133
soul luminous like, 157
two forms of light, 142-145

T

Theory of evolution, xix
thought, 26, 55, 71-74, 88
truth,
always speak, 13
ātmā is, 10
born of, 32
brahma is, 17, 31
left eye, 77
triumps over non-truth, 178

U

un-manifest (*avyakta*), 111, 121, 158n
universe,
brahma pervades, 178
conception of, 138-139
created from chaos, 154, 159
guardian of, 167
protector of, 163
puruṣa is, 150
unreal, see *asat*

V

Varuna, 5, 15, 27, 29, 61
Vedanta, 162n, 182n, 206
Vedas, 11-14, 24-26, 60, 153, 169, 191

W

wealth, 7-8, 101-105, 127, 186n
woman, 34, 41, 58, 114
womb,
access point to world, 154
after death, 117
brahma in, 146
embryo, 42-43
fire, 114
five miseries, 140
move within, 191
of space, 52
three births, 34, 40n

Y

Yama, god of death, 77, 96, 112
yoga, path of, 10

Z

zenith, 187

Ganga Flows West
A Hindu Primer

An easy to read and simple explanation of the most important points of Hinduism.

by Shukavak N. Dasa

"I've seen that ritual a hundred times, this however, is the first time I understood its meaning"

Hindu Encounter with Modernity

Kedarnath Datta Bhaktivinoda, Vaiṣṇava Theologian

Nineteen century India was a time of great religious and cultural change as European religions and philosophies spread throughout the Indian subcontinent. Through the eyes of one Hindu religious reformer, Kedarnath Datta Bhaktivinoda, *Hindu Encounter with Modernity* is a study of how Hinduism evolved and adapted to Western culture and ideas.

Bhaktivinoda's life straddled contemporary British society and ancestral Hindu culture. One was a modern, analytical world which demanded rational thought. The other was a traditional world of Hindu faith and piety, which seemingly allowed little room for critical analysis. Could he play a meaningful role in modern society and at the same time maintain integrity as a Hindu? ISBN 978-1-889756-30-1

www.ingramcontent.com/pod-product-compliance
Lightning Source LLC
Chambersburg PA
CBHW041305110526
44590CB00028B/4250
9781889756042